wired
Beautiful

30+ jewelry projects to hammer, coil, spiral and twist

Heidi Boyd

NORTH LIGHT BOOKS

CINCINNATI, OHIO

D0534086

Wired Beautiful Copyright © 2010 by Heidi Boyd. Manufactured in the United States of America. All rights reserved. No part of this book may be reproduced in any form or by any electronic or mechanical means including information storage and retrieval systems without permission in writing from the publisher, except by a reviewer who may quote brief passages in a review. Published by North Light Books, an imprint of F+W Media, Inc., 4700 East Galbraith Road, Cincinnati, Ohio, 45236. (800) 289-0963. First Edition.

14 13 12 11 10   5 4 3 2 1

DISTRIBUTED IN CANADA BY FRASER DIRECT
100 Armstrong Avenue
Georgetown, ON, Canada L7G 5S4
Tel: (905) 877-4411

DISTRIBUTED IN THE U.K. AND EUROPE BY DAVID & CHARLES
Brunel House, Newton Abbot, Devon, TQ12 4PU, England
Tel: (+44) 1626 323200, Fax: (+44) 1626 323319
Email: postmaster@davidandcharles.co.uk

DISTRIBUTED IN AUSTRALIA BY CAPRICORN LINK
P.O. Box 704, S. Windsor NSW, 2756 Australia
Tel: (02) 4577-3555

Library of Congress Cataloging in Publication Data
Boyd, Heidi
  Wired beautiful : 30+ jewelry projects to hammer, coil, spiral, and twist / by Heidi Boyd. -- 1st ed.
    p. cm.
  Includes index.
  ISBN 978-1-4403-0310-4 (pbk. : alk. paper)
  1. Jewelry making. 2. Wire craft. I. Title.
  TT212.B683 2010
  739.27--dc22
                        2010011644

www.fwmedia.com

Edited by *Julie Hollyday*

Cover by *Marissa Bowers*

Layout Design by *Steven Peters*

Production by *Greg Nock*

Photography by *Christine Polomsky, Ric Deliantoni*

Styling by *Jan Nickum*

METRIC CONVERSION CHART

To convert	to	multiply by
Inches	Centimeters	2.54
Centimeters	Inches	0.4
Feet	Centimeters	30.5
Centimeters	Feet	0.03
Yards	Meters	0.9
Meters	Yards	1.1

DEDICATION

This book was conceived with the encouraging words of Tonia Davenport and Christine Doyle. They realized the need for a modern, comprehensive beginners wire book and trusted me with the challenge. I'm grateful for their vision and confidence in my work. What I hadn't counted on was their matchmaking abilities. In the process of designing these projects, I fell in love with a new medium.

ACKNOWLEDGMENTS

I'm so fortunate to have a team of experts who beautify my work and words. I was thrilled to be back in the photo studio with Christine Polomsky behind the lens. Her years of shooting books have crowned her a craft expert; she resourcefully saved the *Caged Pebbles Pendant* choker with a drop of olive oil. My editor, Julie Hollyday, kept me on track and compiled the vast variety of projects into the book you hold in your hands. I'm thankful for Marissa Bowers and Steven Peters's design savvy. I'm grateful to the talents of Jan Nickum, who helped make any shot a keeper.

Special thanks to Beadalon, Blue Moon Beads, Darice, Clover, Halcraft, Plaid, and Vintaj for graciously providing me with materials and tools that inspire creativity.

On the home front, I'd never get anywhere without my fabulous husband, Jon. Fortunately my family is adept at living in creative chaos. I'm tickled when my teenage sons, Jasper and Elliot, admire a design, and can always count on my daughter, Celia, to be enamored with everything that shines and sparkles.

ABOUT THE AUTHOR

Heidi Boyd is the author of eleven craft books with North Light Books, most notably the Simply Beautiful series. Her goal is to make sophisticated design approachable and easy for all. She has a fine art degree and got her start in professional crafting as a contributor to *Better Homes and Gardens* books and magazines. She contributes to national craft publications and loves teaching craft workshops to children and adults. Heidi; her husband, Jon; and their three children enjoy the natural beauty of their midcoast Maine home.

Please stop by her blog, heidiboyd.blogspot.com, for more project ideas.

CONTENTS

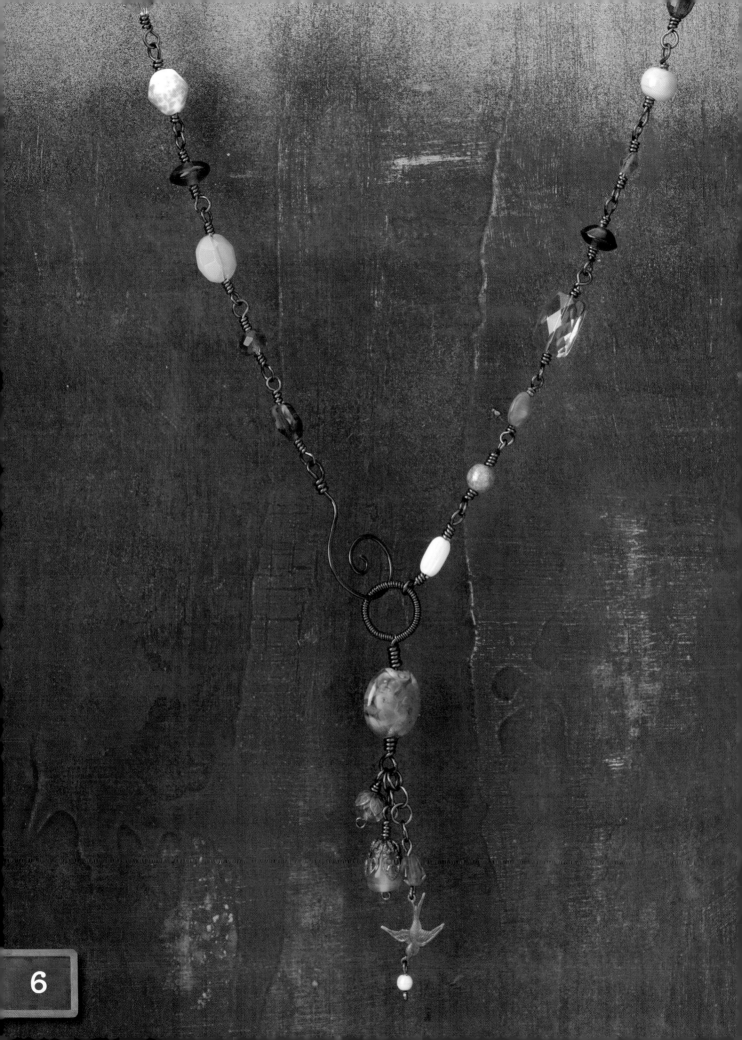

INTRODUCTION

Until recently, I've been guilty of overlooking the wire displays in jewelry supply stores. Like a magpie, I was immediately drawn to the walls of sparkly, glittery beads. With a fistful of beads in hand, selecting stringing wire was almost an afterthought. My final stop would be to scan the jewelry findings racks where I often was unable to find exactly what I needed.

It took a complete shift in my focus to realize that wire could expand the possibilities of my jewelry design. Wire's design possibilities are limitless. A thicker gauge wire can become the core of a bangle, be wrapped into a link or be formed into a toggle clasp. Medium-gauge wires can be shaped into earwires, coiled into jump rings or even wrapped into a bead. Thinner gauge wire is so flexible it can be knitted and crocheted into intricate masterpieces.

Never again will I trek to store after store in search of a simple jump ring clasp or earwire; with wire, I can make them in any color and size I want.

With a single coil of wire and a few tools, you can twist, shape, link and hammer almost any jewelry component and save both time and money.

For starters, you'll need to equip yourself with a few tools. Wirework is very accessible; unlike other metal jewelry work, you won't need a soldering iron, anvil or torch. The basic pliers, a jump ring maker, hammer and bench block are readily available and will easily fit at the end of your worktable. Other user-friendly devices, like wire twisters and coiling gizmos, need only a simple turn of the handle. Go to page 11 to read about the tools you'll need to complete the projects in this book.

Knowing how to select the appropriate wire is the key to your success. The materials lists will help you choose the perfect wire for every task. Each wire variety has its own merits—it's impossible to make a thin wire stronger or a thick wire more flexible—so read through the wire descriptions on page 8 to learn more about them. Every project specifies a certain wire that will not only help you recreate the piece, but also spare you any guesswork or frustration.

And don't forget the beads! Adding beads to wirework can give your jewelry designs a whole new depth, dimension and sparkle. Pair crystals with bright silver wires, or choose ceramic beads to go with darker ones. Lampwork and handmade beads enhance more organic wire designs, while commercially produced beads can still pack a punch with whimsical styles. Page 9 features descriptions of beads perfect for the projects in this book.

On the following pages, I've shared every aspect of my newfound wireworking skills. After you work your way through some of the projects in this book, I hope you share my epiphany: Wire is an integral part of almost every jewelry-making project. It may take a little practice to familiarize your hands with the twists and turns of the basic wirework techniques, but I promise the rewards and sense of accomplishment will make your efforts worthwhile. Your imagination is your only limitation. Wire can be shaped into almost anything, from spiraled hearts to flying birds, while showcasing those beautiful beads!

MATERIALS AND TOOLS

Selecting the appropriate wire for the task is key to your wirework success. Every gauge and variety of wire has inherent strengths and weaknesses. Please take advantage of my careful research (and burgeoning studio waste can) and use the wire that is listed for each project.

WIRES

The first thing to know when you're shopping for wire is the higher number of the gauge, the thinner the wire; conversely, the lower the number of the gauge, the thicker the wire. (It seems counterintuitive, but that's the way it works.) A 32-gauge wire is thinner than thread, and a 12-gauge wire is as thick as some varieties of rope. Popular wire gauges in the 18- to 22-gauge range can be difficult to tell apart.

It's a good idea to tag wire coils when you remove them from their packaging so you can identify exactly what they are. You can also purchase a wire gauge tool at an electrical supply store that will help take the guesswork out of identifying what size wire you have on hand.

After working your way through several projects, you'll notice certain wires are used repeatedly for tasks. For instance, 18-gauge wire is great for making clasps, 20-gauge wire spirals and coils easily to make jump rings, and 24-gauge wire is often used for wrapping.

STRINGING WIRE

Stringing wire is made up of multiple fine wires encased in a protective nylon coating. It comes in a range of thicknesses and colors. The wires' strength and flexibility is determined by the number of core wires, from seven strands to forty-nine strands. These wires can be plated with metals. In this book, the stringing wires usually are paired with conventional metal wires, and, in most cases, the thicker varieties are used.

COPPER WIRE

Natural copper wire can be found in hardware, craft and jewelry supply stores. The copper wire sold in craft and jewelry supply stores has a protective finish that prevents it from tarnishing. The variety sold in hardware stores tarnishes quickly. There are advantages to both varieties: If you're looking for a finished piece that requires little maintenance, use the tarnish-free wire; if you want a dark and aged appearance for your project, use the uncoated wire. Copper wire is great for practicing wireworking techniques.

COLORED COPPER WIRE

This is a permanently colored copper wire, meaning the copper wire has a colored coating that is engineered to resist tarnishing, chipping and peeling. It comes in a huge range of colors and gauges in both high-shine and matte finishes. Beadalon is the expert purveyor of this variety of wire.

GERMAN-STYLE SILVER-PLATED WIRE

This wire is the namesake of Beadalon's silver-plated, antitarnish copper wire product. It's my choice for a sterling silver look without the price. It is the perfect temper (malleability, for us newbies), making it easy to form a variety of shapes, bead links, coils and bead cages and great for all wire-wrapping uses.

STERLING SILVER WIRE

This wire is priced by the ounce and sold by the foot. It comes in different softness levels. I recommend using half-hard in most cases because the more malleable dead-soft can actually be harder to manipulate. Sterling silver wire is also available in other wire shapes, such as squares. As a beginner, select the standard round wire to make a seamless transition from practice pieces made with copper wire.

ALUMINUM WIRE

Just as its name says, this wire is made from aluminum. Very easy to work with, aluminum wire is a great way to get bold pieces into your wirework without the weight or exertion of cutting through traditional heavier metals. Darice manufactures this wire in a wide variety of colors and a few popular gauges.

A NOTE ABOUT THE PROJECTS IN THIS BOOK

This book is made with the beginner in mind; only two earring projects use more expensive sterling silver wire. The majority of the projects are made with plated or coated copper wire. Copper wire has the advantage of being easy to use, affordable and widely available. You can practice a technique over and over again without worrying about the cost. If you're happy with your results and want to make the piece in sterling, by all means please do, just stick with user-friendly half-hard round silver wire.

For the sake of variety I've added some really interesting wires. Black annealed wire is found at the hardware store; the outside coating can be sanded, adding depth to its appearance. New aluminum wire is very soft and light—even the thick 12-gauge makes hefty-looking pieces that are a joy to wear.

BLACK ANNEALED WIRE

Annealed wire is heated, or "burnt," carbon steel wire or iron steel wire. Typically found in hardware stores, it's used in construction and agriculture for baling hay and rebar fencing. Soft annealed wire offers excellent flexibility, making it an inexpensive wire choice that adds a great nontraditional look to your jewelry.

NICKEL WIRE

Nickel silver jewelry wire is an alloy of copper, nickel and sometimes zinc. Found in jewelry supply stores, it is an economical alternative to sterling silver wire. It's highly resistant to corrosion and is very malleable. Like coated copper wire, nickle wire is an excellent practice wire. Take care when choosing this wire for a project because some people have allergic reactions to nickel wire.

BEADS

I can't imagine creating a piece of jewelry without having a selection of beads at hand. Wire and beads are made for each other—in most cases, the wire slips easily through the bead. In this book, wire also wraps, spirals, cages and loops around beads to form stunning pieces of jewelry. The main concern when purchasing beads for wirework is to be aware of the size of the bead openings; some machine-drilled openings can't accommodate anything but the thinnest gauges of wire.

GLASS BEADS

The majority of beads you'll find in stores are made of glass. In its molten form, the glass can be formed into almost any shape. The variety of colors and finishes is just as limitless.

SEED BEADS

These tiny, inexpensive beads are available in a wide range of colors and finishes, including metallic, and they come in a variety of sizes. Traditional seed beads have slightly irregular shapes and openings. Delica seed beads have uniform shapes and sizes. Regardless of which you choose, make sure the beads' openings are large enough to accommodate the selected stringing wire.

E BEADS

These beads are slightly larger than seed beads. They come in a myriad of colors and sizes.

MAGATAMA BEADS

Magatama beads have the same sized opening as E beads, but they have a semiteardrop shape.

CANE BEADS

These beads are glass beads cut from a collection of fused-glass canes. Each bead slice has a cross section of all the cane colors.

LAMPWORK BEADS

Lampwork beads are created one at a time by a skilled artisan who sculpts glass by twirling thin rods of colored glass over a gas-oxygen burner. Many lampwork beads showcase layers of designs and patterns.

RESIN BEADS

Acrylic resin beads are formed in molds. These beads feel slightly heavier than traditional plastic, reminiscent of Bakelite plastic. They often have a lovely frosted appearance similar to tumbled glass.

CERAMIC BEADS

Made with natural clays, ceramic beads are typically finished with layers of glaze. They have a pleasing weight, and the irregularities of the glaze finish make each bead unique.

FRESHWATER PEARLS

Ranging in size from the smallest pearl to an elongated 13mm-long tube shape, pearls add a lovely sheen to any project. The pearls are usually coated with an iridescent finish that highlights their natural irregularities. Pearls tend to have small drilled holes that pose a challenge to wirework; usually only higher gauges will fit through the holes.

STONE AND CHIP BEADS

These beads are often cut from natural and semiprecious stones. They're polished into smooth round, faceted or small chip beads with center-drilled holes. Like pearls, the openings of the smaller stone beads tend to be narrow, allowing them to be strung only by thinner gauged wires or stringing wire.

SHELL BEADS

These natural beads are cut into all different sizes and shapes. Like pearls and stone and chip beads, their stringing holes are machine-drilled, making a thinner gauged wire a necessity. Often they are dyed vibrant colors to enhance the shell's irregularities.

WOODEN BEADS AND LINKS

A resurgence of seventies fashion sensibilities has brought a great new selection of wooden beads and links to the market. Natural wood is a wonderful backdrop for silver metalwork and brings added texture to traditional glass and stone bead pairings.

FELT BEADS

Formed with 100 percent wool fibers, felt beads have enjoyed recent popularity at craft stores. I've yet to see them on display in the bead aisle, so wander down to the needle felting supplies or visit an online retailer to locate them. (If you're interested in making your own felt beads, check out the step-by-step tutorial in *Simply Beaded Bliss*, by yours truly.)

METAL CHARMS

When you find a charm you like, it's a good idea to grab it and add it to your stash. A single charm can be all you need to put the finishing touch on your wirework. Charms come in a variety of metal finishes, shapes and sizes. Manufacturers update their charms and release new ones all the time. The majority of the charms used in this book were made by Plaid.

RUBBER O-RINGS

These flexible circles of rubber integrate beautifully with traditional wire jump rings. Available in a host of colors and sizes, they're just starting to show up in the jewelry aisle. I ordered the ones for the *Stretch Rubber O-Ring Bracelet* from theringlord.com.

CRIMP BEADS AND TUBES

I often use these to attach clasps to stringing wire. Be sure to purchase crimps that will accommodate a double thickness of the selected stringing wire. Use gold, silver, black, copper or antique finishes to match the wire.

METAL GLUE

Twisting and looping wire together form the majority of the jewelry connections in this book. The few times glue is used, it's to hold a bead and metal component together. It's vitally important to use glue formulated exactly for that purpose. I highly recommend Aleene's Jewelry & Metal Glue; it's my favorite for wirework.

TOOLS

Your hands are your very best wirework tools. You need to be careful with them: The constant pressure and poking of the wire ends, especially with thicker wires, will wear on your thumb and fingertips. Second to your hands are pairs of round- and chain-nose pliers. They will not only save your fingertips but will help you firmly grasp and manipulate wire. The third essential tool is a strong, sharp pair of flush cutters.

The following list of tools will help you decide where to invest the rest of your craft dollars. All the tools will help simplify your ability to create with wire. Some tools, such as the jump ring maker, are used in almost all the projects, whereas the wire twister is used for only a few designs. In the end, it comes down to your personal taste and which designs capture your interest. Equip yourself with the tools you need to make the projects that inspire you.

CHAIN-NOSE PLIERS

These pliers have two flat, tapered pincers ideal for wirework. They are perfect for holding the wire while it's being shaped or wrapped. If you have trouble with the pliers marking the wire coating, you can wrap the tips in electrical tape. To cut down on tool investment for beginners, I intentionally substituted chain-nose pliers to squeeze crimps flat instead of using crimping pliers.

ROUND-NOSE PLIERS

These have two smooth, round, tapered pincers that facilitate turning the end of a wire into a round loop. They're also used to form the center of a spiral. In a pinch, one of the round pincers can be used to make a small coil.

FLUSH CUTTERS

These are an essential tool for trimming wire. Scissors are not suited to wirework; it's always safer and easier to make a quick clip with flush cutters than to exert too much pressure with scissor blades. I recommend purchasing two different cutters: standard for cutting wires 19-gauge and thinner; large for cutting heavy wires 18-gauge and lower. Sharp flush cutters will make a smooth cut edge on the wire.

BENT-NOSE PLIERS

The tapered ends of the bent-nose pliers are turned at a 90-degree angle, which allows the pliers to reach into tight areas. Bent-nose pliers are commonly used in conjunction with chain-nose pliers when linking jump rings to create a chain. These pliers help save your fingers and make it easy to apply equal pressure simultaneously to both sides of a jump ring.

NYLON-TIPPED PLIERS

These pliers are specially coated to safely clamp wire and prevent it from being marred. My favorite use for nylon-tipped wires is to pull them down a length of wire to straighten it. While it's a handy tool, nylon-tipped pliers are nonessential to the projects in this book.

JUMP RING MAKER AND JUMP RING MANDREL

These two tools serve the same purpose—making jump rings. But you'll want to choose them according to how many jump rings you want to make.

Beadalon's jump ring maker consists of a clear base outfitted with a nut and a selection of different-sized metal bars that screw into the base. You coil the wire up the selected bar to make multiple jump rings. You can buy additional kits to make very large rings and even oval-shaped rings.

Jump ring mandrels feature multiple separate, tapered metal bars with a padded handle. The tips of each mandrel are divided into $1/2$" (1.5cm) sections graduated from large to small. You simply wrap the wire around the desired section to make the coil for the jump rings. Again, I like the version produced by Beadalon. Although this is a quick and handy tool, it doesn't lend itself to making the quantity of jump rings that the jump ring maker does.

RING MANDREL

A ring mandrel is a tapered form you use to wrap wire into a ring shape. It can be made of wood or metal, and most mandrels are marked with lines to indicate ring sizes. I love the lightweight simplicity of wood mandrels. By placing one of my rings on the mandrel, I quickly determine where to wrap the wire to make the same size ring. I also use it to make larger round shapes with wire.

JEWELER'S HAMMER

A jeweler's hammer is unlike a standard hammer in the toolbox. The flat end with smooth, rounded edges is called the planishing side; the other side is a small, round ball, called the ball peen. The planishing side is used to harden shaped wire, while the smooth edges help prevent the hammer from denting or marking your piece. The ball-peen side is ideal for creating dimpled patterns on wirework. Store your hammer carefully, and don't let anyone use it for handiwork around the house.

BENCH BLOCK

This is used in conjunction with the jeweler's hammer. Bench blocks are sold in different sizes; a small one should meet your needs for all the designs in this book. The block provides a stable surface that will support your jewelry piece while it's being hammered. (You can't substitute plastic or wooden boards, because the metal hammer and jewelry will indent and break them.) Hammering on the bench block is loud. Some jewelry makers use sewn suede "bench bags" filled with metal BBs to deaden the sound and hold the block in place, but I've found foam gardener's knee pads work well under the block.

COILING GIZMO

The Coiling Gizmo makes coiling wire a snap. It comes with a base piece that can be screwed directly into your worktable or onto a separate block of wood. There are two pairs of different-sized holes in the top of the base piece, and two corresponding-sized rods. You can select either a thin or thick rod depending on what size coil you're making. The Coiling Gizmo is used for two projects in this book, but it's easy to use to create your own jewelry designs.

WIRE TWISTER

This tool makes twisting multiple lengths of wire together a breeze. Use this twisted wire to make twisted jump rings and other jewelry components for added texture. You can achieve the same results with a drill, but I like the simplicity and ease of the Beadalon ColourCraft Wire Twister. It's easy to stop and make any necessary adjustments.

FILES

Files are important to wire jewelry work because they allow your jewelry to be snag-free and comfortable to wear. It is especially important to file the part of the earwire that goes through the ear. You'll want a variety of files, from coarser to finer files. I like the file set made by Vintaj; they're perfectly sized for wire jewelry work, and the files are color-coded and linked together, making them easy to find and use.

SANDING STICKS

I found these ready-made files at a local jewelry supply store. They're basically fine grits of sandpapers that have been wrapped around a wooden stick. They are the perfect follow-up to metal files.

SANDING SPONGES

Sanding sponges are widely available at hardware stores, and, like sandpapers, they come in a variety of grits. These sponges are easy to work with and are ideal for use with black annealed wire.

JEWELRY POLISHING CLOTHS

Use these for the perfect shine every time! Always give your piece a rub with a polishing cloth. One side removes the dirt; the other side makes the piece shine. They are available almost anywhere jewelry is sold. If you're using uncoated copper, a jewelry cloth is a must to keep the natural tarnishing under control.

TIP

Consider both the size and quality of the tools you purchase. Mini plier sets can be handy for thin wirework and bead stringing, but they do not have the strength to handle cutting or manipulating wires thicker than 20-gauge. I can't stress how important it is to invest in quality standard-sized tools, especially for the essential pliers and flush cutters. Good tools will help eliminate frustration and make it easier to learn and master wirework techniques.

TECHNIQUES

If you're brand-new to wire jewelry making, make this section your first stop on your wirework adventure. If you already have some experience working with wire, you might be surprised to find a new trick or shortcut in the following pages. As you work your way through the projects in the book, you'll find yourself flipping back to this section. Here you'll find frequently used techniques, such as making earring wires, spirals and wrapped links. Mark these pages so you can quickly get back to them when needed.

Many tips, such as properly cutting wire and compressing coiled wires, are shown here and are not always called out in the individual instructions. To give your work a more professional finish, be sure to look over the hammering, sanding and polishing information on page 21.

TIP
Grab a length of wire and your basic tools to try your hand at coiling jump rings and making your own clasps. If you experience any difficulties, simply switch to a different gauge or variety of wire. Both lighter gauges (18 and higher) and nonplated wires are easier to manipulate. After you've gotten a feel for the technique with the new wire, try it again with the original wire; it should be easier.

MAKING EARWIRES

I still can't believe how easy it is to shape earwires. A single spool of wire can make countless pairs of earrings. The best part is you can easily customize the wire thickness, color and shape to work with your design ideas.

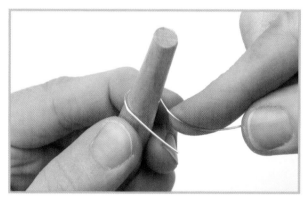

1 Wrap the wire around the small end of the ring mandrel. Cut the back wire so it's 1½" (4cm) long.

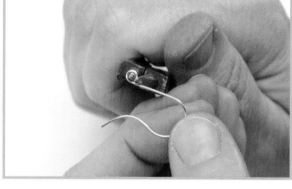

2 Use chain-nose pliers to make a bend in the last ¼" (6mm) of the wire. Grab the front end of the earwire with the round-nose pliers and turn it into a loop to connect the dangle.

3 Gently hammer the shaped earwire to harden the metal.

4 Carefully sand the exposed cut wire end smooth so it can gently thread through the earlobe.

MAKING JUMP RINGS

I can't tell you how much money and time I've wasted buying the "right" jump ring for a project. After you realize how easy they are to make, you will never fall into this trap. Using a jump ring mandrel or jump ring maker and flush cutters, you can make custom jump rings in minutes. The same basic technique is used regardless of the wire gauge or size of the ring.

1 Screw the desired sized metal bar into the base. Hook the wire end into the base. You can substitute a jump ring mandrel; just select the appropriate millimeter section to wrap.

2 Tightly coil the desired amount of wire; one full rotation makes one jump ring.

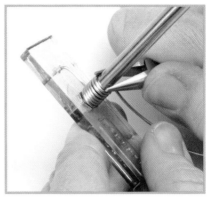

3 Push down on the top of the coils to compress them.

4 Using the flush cutters, trim the wire tail holding the coils to the base and slide the coil off the jump ring maker.
   Using the flush cutters, trim off the excess wire tail.

5 Cut the rings apart, working your way from the bottom of the coil up to the top. Position the cuts one on top of the other.

6 If the cutting process compresses the wire end, recut it (see Basic Wire Finishing on page 20). The finished ring should have flat ends and retain the round shape of the bar or mandrel.

OPENING AND CLOSING JUMP RINGS

It's vitally important to learn how to properly open and close jump rings. If you pull the wire ends apart, you'll not only distort the round shape, but you'll also lose the tension of the coiled wire.

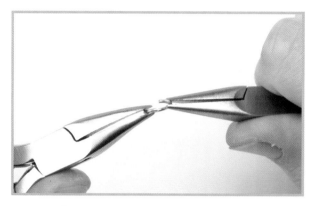

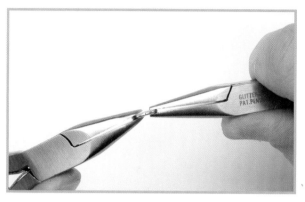

1 Using bent-nose pliers and chain-nose pliers (or two pairs of chain-nose pliers, as shown here), grasp the jump ring on either side of its cut opening. Open the ring by moving one pair of pliers toward you and one away from you, in a scissor-like fashion.

2 Hook the ring through the desired components and use the pliers to securely close the ring in the same manner described in step 1. You'll hear and feel a click when the ends reconnect.

COMPRESSING A COIL

Any time you wrap or coil wire, it must be uniform and shouldn't have any gaps.

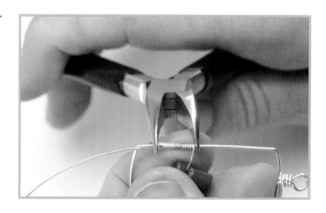

1 When wrapping wire around a thicker wire base, use the bent-nose pliers to squeeze the wrapped wire together, eliminating any irregular spacing.

When using the Coiling Gizmo, it's easy to exert pressure by pushing the wire rod against the base.

MAKING A SPIRAL

Spirals have a multitude of clever uses: They make a decorative wire end, they can be an integral part of a functioning clasp or they can make a beautiful link. It takes a little time to get comfortable making freeform spirals. Start with flexible wire and work your way up to thicker gauges. After some practice, you should be ready to incorporate spirals into your necklace and bracelet projects.

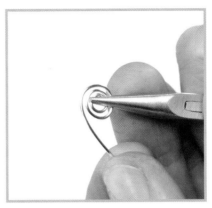

1 Usually spirals are made directly off the spool because it is hard to determine how much wire you'll need. Make sure the end of the wire has a straight, clean cut. Grab the wire end in the round-nose pliers. Use your other hand to rotate the wire tightly around the secured end.

2 After making 2 rotations, slip the round-nose pliers out of the center of the spiral. Clamp the spiral in the chain-nose pliers (or nylon-tipped pliers). Continue wrapping the wire around the outside of the center spiral, rotating the spiral piece in the pliers as needed.

3 Trim the wire to the desired length to finish the component. For added stability, hammer the finished spiral on the block.

MAKING AN S-LOOP/LINK

The S-loop is simply two connected spirals. The size of the spirals can be increased by making additional rotations or decreased by making fewer rotations. The following hanging loop has a larger end to accommodate the necklace and a smaller end to hook on to the finished pendant. When modifying the steps for an S-link, increase the length of the wire and create tighter, balanced spirals on both ends.

1 Cut a 3" (7.5cm) length of wire. Grasp one end of the wire with the round-nose pliers. Create the larger side of the loop by making a full wire rotation around the trapped end.

2 Release the finished side and grasp the other end of the wire in the pliers. Make the small side of the S-shape by tightly circling the wire around in the opposite direction.

3 Hammer the shaped wire to harden the metal.

MAKING WRAPPED LINKS

Wrapped links elegantly frame a bead while forming a strong connecting link. The wire creates a wrapped loop on one side and then spirals around the bead before wrapping back around the original loop. The technique can easily be modified to make a decorative dangle as seen in the *Spiraled Resin Bracelet* (page 112). This versatile link can be used with different kinds of beads and wire for necklace and bracelet projects. You'll be instructed in each project about what starting wire length you'll need.

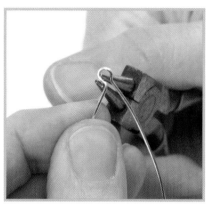

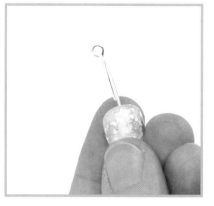

1 Starting 1" (2.5cm) from the wire end, use round-nose pliers to shape the wire into a loop.

2 Use the pliers to pinch each wire at the base of the loop and bend them out.

3 Push the wire tails together and slide the bead onto the wires. Push the bead up so it sits below the loop. The other wire end should now be hidden inside the bead.

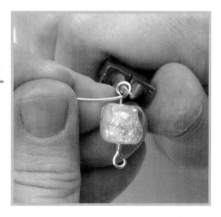

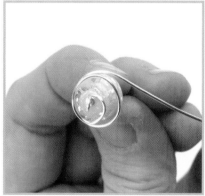

4 Use the round-nose pliers to form another loop on the other side of the bead. Wrap the wire around the base of the loop to stabilize it.

5 Spiral the wire around the bead, increasing and decreasing the wraps to contour to the bead's shape.

6 Spiral the wire around the base of the first loop and then use the flush cutters to trim away the excess wire. Use the chain-nose pliers to pinch the wire end flush with the base of the wire loop.

If you're making a chain of links, hook the new link through a loop of the first link (step 4) before you wrap and spiral the wire.

CRIMPING STRINGING WIRE

This basic stringing technique should be the first jewelry technique you learn. Crimping takes the place of knotting; it's regularly used to attach clasps to the end of a beaded strand. A crimp bead is essentially a small wire tube strung onto a cabled stringing wire. When you squeeze the crimp with chain-nose or crimping pliers, the flattened metal traps the stringing wire in place.

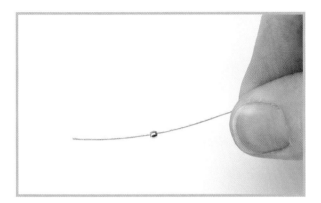

1 String a crimp bead onto the stringing wire.

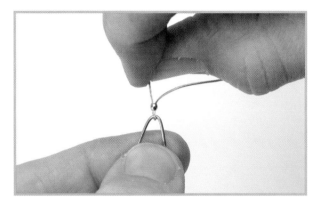

2 Pass the stringing wire through the wire component. String the stringing wire back through the crimp bead. Pull through any slack stringing wire and push the bead down flush against the clasp or wire component.

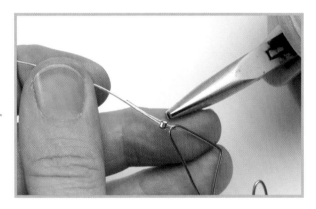

3 Use the chain-nose pliers to squeeze the crimp flat.

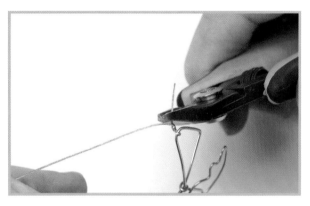

4 Trim the excess wire with flush cutters.

A double-thick wire hook is obviously stronger than its single-thickness counterpart. It's a great way to adapt a thinner wire, which you might already have on hand from linking or wrapping the length of the project, into a functioning clasp. When using thicker wire, you can simply modify these steps to make a single-wire version of both the hook and ring. Many times the hook can be used alone and simply attached to the last ring of a chain necklace or bracelet.

DOUBLE HOOK CLASP

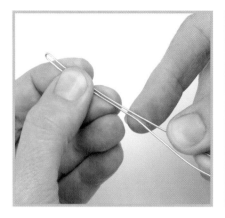

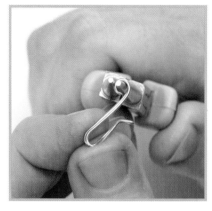

1 Cut a 4" (10cm) length of wire and fold it in half.

2 Fold ½" (1.5cm) of the folded wire end over the round-nose pliers to create the top of the hook.

3 Use the chain-nose pliers to slightly bend the last ¼" (6mm) of the hook upward. Wrap the other end of the wire around the round-nose pliers to shape a connecting loop at the base of the hook.

DOUBLE O-RING

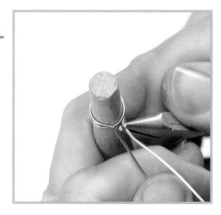

1 Wrap a 2½" (6.5cm) piece of wire around the small end of the ring mandrel or a wide jump ring shaft two times. (You can shape it into a square, a triangle, an oval or any other closed shape you can think of.) Bend the wires at a 90-degree angle out from the base of the ring.

2 Use the round-nose pliers to shape one of the wire ends into a connecting loop.

3 Trap the connecting loop in the chain-nose pliers while you wrap the second wire around the O-ring and the connecting loop. Trim both wire ends with flush cutters.

BASIC WIRE FINISHING

Take a quick read through the following finishing tips to become familiar with how the tools and materials are used to make your wirework creations shine.

TRIMMING WIRE ENDS

Flush cutters can compress wires when you make the first cut. To get a clean, flush cut, you may need to recut the wire end. This extra step is worth the effort because it gives your finished piece a more professional appearance and prevents the wire from snagging on clothing and irritating the wearer.

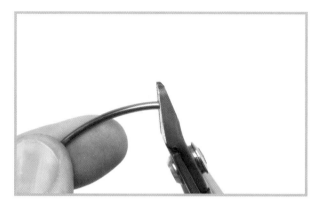

1 This thick aluminum wire clearly illustrates how the wire has become compressed, giving the cut end a diagonal appearance.

2 Face the flat side of the flush cutters toward the wire length and recut the tip of the wire.

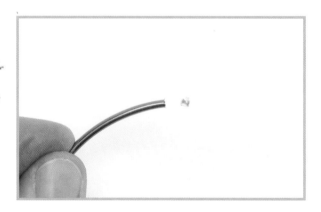

3 The new end should be straight and flush. If you're still having trouble, your flush cutters may be dull or not strong enough to properly cut through the wire.

HAMMERING METAL COMPONENTS

Hammering metal pieces strengthens the individual pieces and, in turn, makes the entire piece of jewelry stronger.

Use the flat (planishing) end of the hammer to harden the components. Hammer on the wrong side in case the hammer leaves marks. You don't need to exert a lot of pressure. Reserve your strength for wire gauges lower than 18 because they can withstand more hits. The ball-peen side of the hammer can be used to give the piece a decorative, dimpled appearance. A leather BB-filled bench block bag under the block will help control sound; a gardening kneeling cushion is an easy-to-find alternative.

USING FILES, SANDING SPONGES AND SANDING STICKS

Filing and sanding wire give your jewelry a finished look and prevent the wire from catching on clothing and poking the wearer.

After the piece is finished, check it for scratches, pliers indentations and rough edges. Where necessary, apply light pressure and sand the marks smooth. Use the finest files, sanding sticks or sanding sponges last. You should always sand the end of the earwire that goes through the ear. You should not sand coated or plated wires, because you will remove the finish.

POLISHING METAL

Polishing cloths are the best way to keep your wirework clean and shiny. They quickly wipe away fingerprints and grime and are essential to have on hand if you're using wire that isn't tarnish resistant. Always polish your finished piece to make it look its best.

Polishing metal pieces is fast and easy. Using a clean cloth, rub the metal piece until it shines.

Chapter 1

WRAPPED AND HAMMERED

Wire can wrap better then any other craft material—it immediately mimics the contour of what it encircles, and unlike fibers, it stays in place without knots or glue. Wire wrapping can be used countless ways to bind, decorate and strengthen your jewelry designs. This chapter is a great place to start exploring basic wrapping techniques.

Wrapping wire with wire adds visual interest and creates a stronger link. The *Wrapped Hoop Necklace* (page 24) is a great example: A single circle of 24-gauge wire will bend easily, but four to five wrapped hoops of the same wire form a viable link. Wrapping multiple objects together with wire will bind them together instantly, like in the *Caged Pebbles Pendant* (page 27). The same principal is at work in the *Wired Cuff* (page 30), although in this case, the beads have the added stability of being strung and then wrapped.

Hammering wire plays an equally vital role in jewelry making. You hammer wire for two main purposes: structural and decorative. Tapping a wire piece a few times hardens the metal so it retains the shape, an approach frequently used when making earrings and clasps. Repeatedly hammering a wire piece with the ball-peen side of the jeweler's hammer decoratively dimples the wire, while the planishing side is used to flatten wire. In *Three Peas in a Pod* (page 43), the flattened wire holds beads in place.

Combining wrapping and hammering doubles the texture and strength in any piece. In the *Copper Links* and *Stone Chip Necklace* (page 40), the links are jeweler's hammered and then decoratively wrapped with a thinner gauge of wire. The *Black Annealed Wire Bead Necklace* (page 35) features wire beads made with thin-gauge wire wound over a hammered, double-eye pin base; the spiraled beads in the same necklace feature hammered wire for a textured look.

Grab your tools and supplies to make some jewelry with beautiful textures. Before you know it, you'll be alternating between wrapping and hammering with ease.

WRAPPED HOOP NECKLACE

If you look closely at this necklace, you'll see it is basically a chain of small wrapped wire hoops. While I was sorting through my wire stash, I took a second look at the wrapped hoops and realized they have a pleasing design—but even more important, the wraps strengthened thin wire. Prestringing the wire with glass lentil beads, wood disks and E or seed beads made the hoops even more interesting.

MATERIALS

18-gauge silver-colored wire

26-gauge German-style silver-plated wire (Beadalon)

5 10mm sapphire silver foil millefiori glass lentils (Halcraft)

3 9mm wooden disk beads (Blue Moon)

11 red E beads

24 turquoise seed beads

TOOLS

ring mandrel

jump ring maker with 8mm mandrel

round-nose pliers

chain-nose pliers

bent-nose pliers

flush cutters

jeweler's hammer

bench block

Finished length: 17" (43cm)

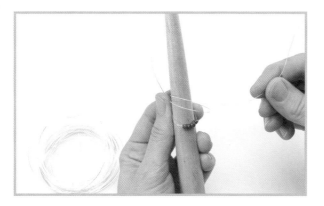

1 You will work directly from the spool of 26-gauge wire. String the desired beads onto the wire. (I used one of four combinations for each hoop: a single sapphire glass lentil, a single wooden disk, 3 red E beads, or 8 turquoise seed beads.) Slide the beads down the wire so they're about a 5" (13cm) from the wire end.

Wrap the beaded wire 5–8 times around the wide end of the mandrel, making sure all the beads are trapped in the loops (this should make approximately 1" [2.5cm] sized loops).

2 Carefully slide the loops off the mandrel, trapping them in your pinched fingertips. Cut 2" (5cm) of wire off the spool with the flush cutters. Tightly wrap the cut end 6–8 times around the wire loops.

3 Repeat steps 1 and 2 to make 5 more 1" (2.5cm) large loops. Use the center of the mandrel to make six ¾" (2cm) hoops. Make four ½" (1.5cm) hoops using the small end of the mandrel.

Arrange the hoops on the work surface. Place the 6 large hoops in the center of the necklace; add 3 medium hoops on each side of the large hoops and then add 2 small hoops on both ends.

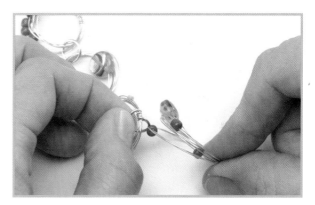

4 Make 15 jump rings using the 18-gauge wire and the 8mm jump ring maker mandrel (see Making Jump Rings on page 14).

Connect the hoops by stringing a jump ring through several open beaded wires of one hoop and then linking it through the wrapped portion of another hoop (see Opening and Closing Jump Rings on page 15).

Repeat this step until the entire strand is connected.

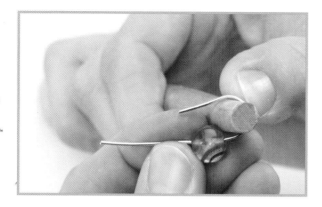

5 To make the clasp, cut a 1¾" (4.5cm) length of 18-gauge wire. String a lentil bead on the center of the wire. Use the mandrel to shape one end into a curved hook. Use the round-nose pliers to bend the very end of the hook back up.

6 Use the round-nose pliers to shape the other end into a small loop.

7 Hammer both ends of the hook. Carefully open the small loop and use the chain-nose pliers to link it to the last wrapped hoop. The curved hook should hook and unhook onto the last wrapped hoop on the other side of the necklace.

CAGED PEBBLES PENDANT

Around my neck of the woods, people often erect cairns by carefully stacking rocks on top of each other to make a mountain or to mark a spot in the woods or beach. I love how the caged wire pendant holds a stack of three small pebbles in the same formation. The wire cage and wrapping technique is so versatile it will easily contour any item; tumbled glass or shells would work equally as well. I strung the memory wire necklace through a black rubber sleeve to make a simple necklace for this intricate pendant.

MATERIALS

18-gauge silver-colored wire
16" (40.5cm) length of 22-gauge silver ColourCraft wire
24-gauge silver-colored wire
3 smooth pebbles
memory wire necklace (Remembrance by Beadalon)
1.7mm black rubber tubing
2 memory-wire end caps
Aleene's Jewelry & Metal Glue

TOOLS

round-nose pliers
flush cutters
jeweler's hammer
bench block

Finished pendant length: 2¼" (6cm)

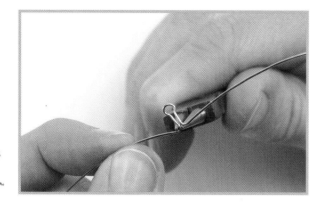

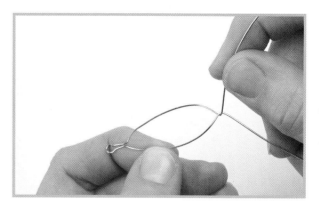

1   Using the flush cutters, cut an 18" (46cm) piece of 22-gauge silver-colored wire. Use round-nose pliers to form a loop in the center of the wire. Use the pliers to bend the wire tails out. Pinch the wire tails together. About ¼" (6mm) from the first bends, bend the wire tails at a 90-degree angle opposite each other.

2   Shape the wires into curved pod sides and then twist the wires together to form the base of the pendant. (Test the base to make sure it is large enough to snugly fit the largest pebble.)

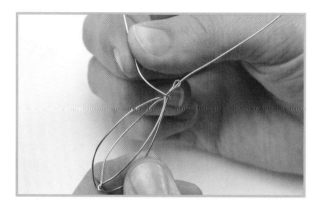

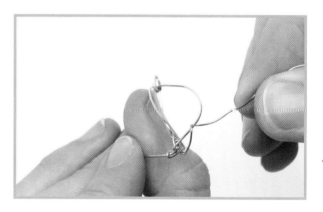

3   Fold the wires back up and shape them into 2 more pod sides. Leave 1 wire straight up against the hanging loop. Wrap the other end 4 times around all 3 wires. Trim the excess wires.

4   Attach a 36" (91.5cm) 24-gauge silver-colored wire at the bottom of the pod by tightly wrapping it where the 22-gauge wires meet. Pull the 24-gauge wire up slightly and wrap it once around one of the pod sides.

5   Continue wrapping the wire around each side and corner of the pod, wrapping and moving the wire up the length of the pod. When you reach about halfway up the pod, add the pebbles to the interior of the pod.

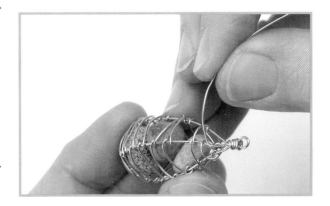

6 Complete the wrap around the pod. When you reach the top of the pod, secure the 24-gauge wire by wrapping it several times around the 18-gauge wire. Trim the excess wire with the flush cutters.

7 Form a hanging S-loop with the 18-gauge wire (see Making an S-Loop/Link on page 16). Connect it to the top of the caged pendant.

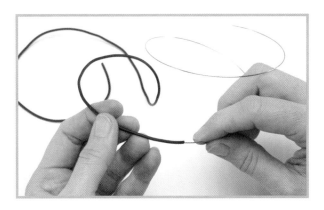

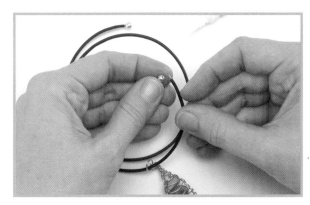

8 Using the flush cutters, cut the memory wire to 18" (46cm). Cut the rubber tubing slightly shorter than 17½" (44.5cm). String the memory wire into the tubing.

9 Slide the pendant to the center of the finished necklace. Glue the silver end caps to the wire ends with the glue. Allow the glue to dry thoroughly before wearing the necklace.

TIP

If you're having trouble sliding the rubber tubing over the wire, add a drop of olive oil to your thumb and pointer finger and grease the wire. The rubber tubing will slide right on.

WIRED CUFF

Everyone who sees this cuff picks it up for a closer look. Tucked inside the wire wraps are a bright mix of colored stone beads. Beads are simply strung onto the wire, and then the wire is tightly wrapped around a blank cuff, making this the perfect wire project for a beginner. The wire forms both the connection and a decorative framework for the beads.

MATERIALS

Silver cuff blank (Plaid)

22-gauge silver-colored copper wire

4 orange stone chips

2 yellow stone chips

2 3mm round turquoise beads

4 6mm round pink jade beads

3 6mm round purple stone beads

2 10mm flat faceted green stone beads

2 10mm flat faceted turquoise beads

Aleene's Jewelry & Metal Glue (optional)

TOOLS

round-nose pliers
flush cutters

Finished wrapped area: 4¾" (12cm)

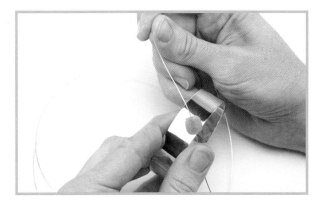

1 Cut 1½ yards (1.5m) of 22-gauge silver-colored wire. Choose a focal bead from one of the larger beads; string it onto one end of the wire and slid it to the middle of the wire. Position the bead over the center front of the cuff and tightly wrap each wire end around the back of the cuff.

2 Wrap both wire ends a second time around the cuff so there is a plain wire on each side of the focal bead. From this point, you'll work with one wire end; let the other end hang down until you're ready to complete the other side of the cuff.

3 String a single round or chip bead onto the active wire end. Slide the bead down the wire so it rests against the cuff. Tightly wrap the wire around the back of the cuff and then make an additional plain wire wrap. Continue tightly wrapping beads onto one side of the cuff. Leave the last quarter of the cuff uncovered and let the wire end hang.

Pick up the wire on the other side of the focal bead and repeat this step on the other side of the cuff. Line up the stopping point with the other side.

4 Working with one wire at a time, wrap the wire ends to cover the beads along the length of the beaded portion of the cuff. Do not add beads.

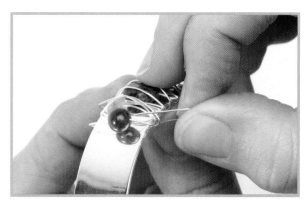

TIP

To ensure good balance, carefully distribute colors, shapes and sizes of the beads across the front of the cuff. Try to avoid positioning the same kinds of beads alongside each other.

5 Use the round-nose pliers to bend the very end of the wire and tuck it into a bead. Repeat for the other wire end. If necessary, add a drop of metal glue to anchor the wire ends in place.

WRAPPED DROP STONE EARRINGS

W**rapping** the top of stone or pearl beads is a fabulous wire technique to master. It allows you to transform plain top-drilled beads into an eye-catching charm, pendant or earrings. The freeform wire wraps mirror the irregular shapes of the natural stone beads. As long as the wire can thread through the stone bead, the subtle differences are not important—they're what make the earrings uniquely handcrafted.

MATERIALS

20-gauge silver-colored wire
24-gauge silver-colored wire
2 6mm 20-gauge wire jump rings (see page 14)
4 top-drilled colored stone beads

TOOLS

ring mandrel
round-nose pliers
chain-nose pliers
bent-nose pliers
flush cutters
jeweler's hammer
bench block
sanding stick
Finished length: 1" (2.5cm)

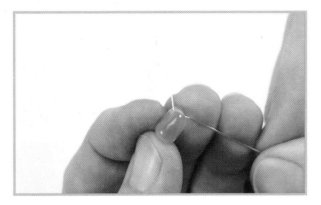

1 Working directly from the spool of 24-gauge wire, pass the wire through the top of the stone bead 1/2" (1.5cm). Bend the 1/2" (1.5cm) wire end up so it sticks straight out the top of the bead.

2 Wrap the other end of the wire around the round-nose pliers to form a loop.

3 Start wrapping the wire around the base of the loop, trapping the wire end in the wraps.

4 Continue wrapping the wire down around the top of the bead, concealing the wired hole. When you're pleased with the wrapping, wrap twice more around the top of the wrap. Cut the wire off the spool with the flush cutters. Tuck the end of the wire into the wire wrap.

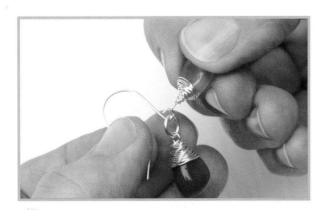

5 Repeat steps 1–4 to wrap the 3 remaining stones. Form 2 earwires with the 20-gauge wire (see Making Earwires on page 13). Link a jump ring to the hanging loop of one of the wrapped stones (see Opening and Closing Jump Rings on page 15). Open the hanging loop of the earwire; add the loaded jump ring and the second stone before closing the loop. Repeat for the matching earring.

BLACK ANNEALED WIRE BEAD NECKLACE

This project incorporates stunning glass resin and stone bead components, pulled together with black annealed wire. Black annealed wire is sold in hardware stores, and it comes in several gauges. Its unique feature is the outer black finish that can be distressed with a sanding sponge: Only the outer wires are sanded to shine silver, while the underlying nooks and crannies all remain black. It's an effective trick that gives your wirework an aged look while avoiding a chemical mess.

MATERIALS

19-gauge black annealed wire

28-gauge black annealed wire

13 6mm jump rings made with 19-gauge black annealed wire (see page 14)

2 lime-green rectangular stone beads

1 orange rectangular resin bead

1 faux topaz acrylic bead

16 4mm tan and brown round faceted beads

2 green glass disks (Plaid)

5 orange ceramic tubes

4 10mm round brown beads

2 10mm green faceted beads

1 resin bird charm (fresh by Plaid)

1 orange glass rectangle (Plaid)

TOOLS

jump ring maker with 7mm mandrel

chain-nose pliers

round-nose pliers

bent-nose pliers

flush cutters

jeweler's hammer

bench block

sanding sponge

Finished length: 23½" (57cm)

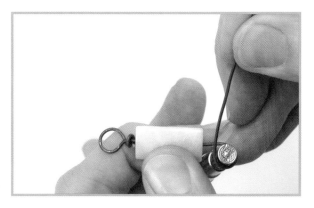

1 Begin by wrapping a large lime-green stone with the annealed wire: Cut an 8" (20.5cm) length of 19-gauge black annealed wire. To form one end into a loop, wrap it around the jump ring maker. To secure the loop, trap it in the chain-nose pliers while you twist the wire end around itself twice at the base of the loop; trim any excess wire.

String the bead onto the open wire end. Use the jump ring maker to form another loop where the wire emerges from the bead. Trap the new loop in the chain-nose pliers while you wrap the wire around itself at the base of the loop.

2 Hammer the remaining length of wire flat on the work surface.

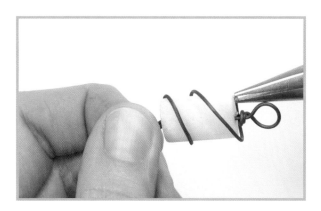

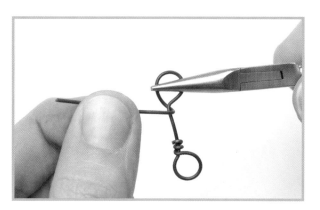

3 Spiral the flattened wire down the length of the bead. Use the chain-nose pliers to wrap the end of the wire around the base of the first loop. Use the sanding sponge to highlight the spiraled wires.

Repeat steps 1–3 to wrap another lime-green stone, an orange resin bead and a faux topaz bead for a total of 4 wrapped beads.

4 To make the wire beads, begin with a 4" (10cm) 19-gauge wire section. As you did in step 1, use the jump ring maker and chain-nose pliers to form one end into a wrapped loop. Leave a ½" (1.5cm) of straight wire, and create a second wrapped loop, winding the excess wire down the straight center section.

5   Cut a 2½' (2.5m) section of 28-gauge wire and wrap one end of it around the center of the wrapped loops. After the end is secure, string four 4mm faceted beads onto the other end of the wire. Continue wrapping the wire, changing directions and positioning the beads to create a round shape. The last 6" (15cm) of wire should be bead-free so the last wraps securely overlap the beads and integrate them into the ball. Bend the very end of the wire down at a 90-degree angle and push it into the wire bead.

6   Use the sanding sponge to lighten the outer wires of the finished wire bead.

Repeat steps 4–6 to make 3 more beads.

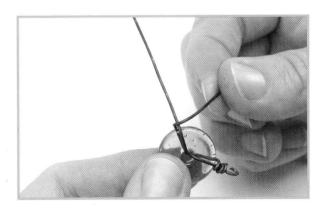

7   Fold a 4" (10cm) section of 19-gauge wire in half and then thread it through the center of the green glass disk. Wrap one wire 3 times around the other wire at the outside edge of the glass disk. Trim the excess wire. Repeat for the opposite side.

8   Use the round-nose pliers to shape the second wire into a loop. Trim away any excess wire.

Repeat steps 7 and 8 to create a single loop around the second green disk.

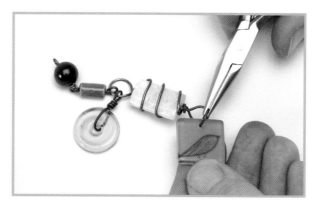

9 Cut twelve 1½" (4cm) sections of 19-gauge wire for the beaded links. Use the round-nose pliers to turn one end of a wire section into a loop. String an orange ceramic tube bead, round brown bead or faceted green bead onto the wire and then turn the other end into a loop. Trim away any excess wire. Repeat this process using all the small beads to make a total of 12 beaded links.

10 Select one of the spiral-wrapped lime-green stone beads as the center of the necklace. Use a jump ring to hang the resin charm from one of its loops and then hook the single-looped green disk and two beaded links from the loop on the other side (see Opening and Closing Jump Rings on page 15).

11 Arrange the remaining large components—3 spiral wrapped beads, 4 wire beads and the double-looped green glass disk—on either side of the focal point. Use two jump rings to link the beads.

12 Link the remaining 11 beaded links to either side of the necklace.

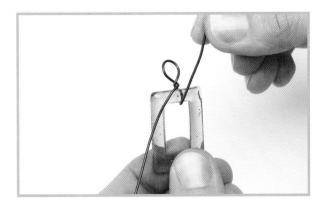

13 To make the clasp, wrap the center of a 6" (15cm) wire section around the jump ring maker. Twist the base of the loop together and then wrap the remaining wire ends around the short side of the orange glass rectangle.

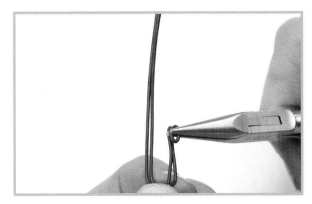

14 To make the hook, fold an 8" (20.5cm) section of 19-gauge wire in half. Use chain-nose pliers to make a square-shaped hook. Use the round-nose pliers to turn up the end of the hook.

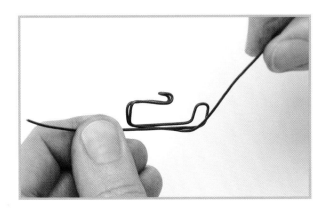

15 Separate the wires at the base of the hook. Form a loop with one of the wires and then use the second wire to wrap the loop end in place. Trim away the excess wire.

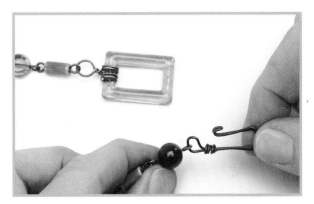

16 Link each clasp component to the last beaded link on either side of the necklace.

COPPER LINKS AND STONE CHIP NECKLACE

The intrinsic beauty of this necklace can be fully appreciated only when it's worn. The repeated scallops of wire fall beautifully around the neckline. The bent links are easily formed with gentle thumb pressure, jeweler's hammer and then decoratively wrapping with fine-gauge wire. The brightly colored stone chips complement the copper, and the attractive flower-shaped clasp could be worn in the front or back.

MATERIALS

18-gauge copper wire

24-gauge copper wire

.018 19-strand satin copper stringing wire (Beadalon)

15–21 brightly colored stone chips (Blue Moon)

4 10mm × 8mm pearl beads

copper crimp beads

TOOLS

round-nose pliers

chain-nose pliers

flush cutters

jeweler's hammer

bench block

Finished length: 16" (40.5cm)

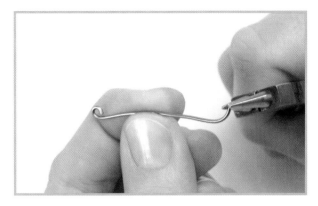

1 Cut three 1½" (4cm) lengths of 18-gauge wire to make the short links. Cut three 2" (5cm) lengths of 18-gauge wire for the long links. Starting with one wire link, use the round-nose pliers to turn one end into a loop. Repeat the process with the other end of the link. Continue curling up both ends of each wire link.

2 Push your thumb into the center of each link to shape it into a curve. Hammer all the links to harden the metal and set their shape (see Basic Wire Finishing on page 20).

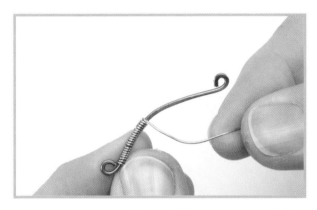

3 Working directly off the spool of 24-gauge wire, tightly wrap the length of a curved link from one loop all the way down to the other loop. Cut the wire off the spool and use the chain-nose pliers to press the cut end firmly against the link. Repeat the process with all the curved links.

4 Using the 18-gauge wire, make 3 S-links with spiral ends (see Making an S-Loop/Link on page 16). Working directly off the spool of 24-gauge wire, tightly wrap the center of each link. Cut the wire off the spool and use the chain-nose pliers to press the cut end firmly against the spiral.

5 Lay out the components in three repetitions of the following sequence: long link, 2–3 stone chips, short link, pearl bead, S-link, 2–3 stone chips. Use 2" (5cm) pieces of copper stringing wire and the copper crimp beads to connect the beaded sections to the wire links (see Crimping Stringing Wire on page 18).

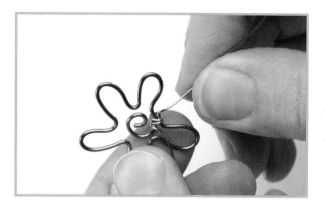

6 To make the flower section of the clasp, work directly from the spool of 18-gauge wire. Grasp the wire end with the round-nose pliers. Rotate the wire once around the pliers' ends as though you were making a spiral and then move the pliers to bend the wire at a 90-degree angle (this creates the base of the first petal). Approximately ½" (1.5cm) up, pinch the wire with the round-nose pliers and bend the wire around the round-nose pliers to make the first petal. Repeat the pinch-and-bend technique to create a total of 5 petals.

7 Cut the wire ¼" (6mm) from the end of the last petal. Position the petals in the desired configuration and hammer the bent wire. Use the 24-gauge wire to tightly wrap the cut wire end to the top of the spiral to connect the petals.

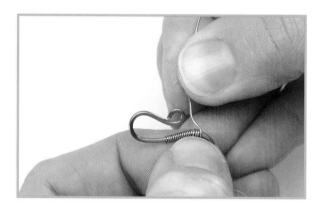

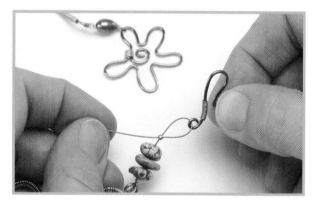

8 Using a 2" (5cm) length of 18-gauge wire, make a hook (see Making Hook and O-Ring Clasps on page 19). Hammer the hook to harden the wire. Wrap the center portion of the hook with 24-gauge wire. Cut the wire off the spool and use the chain-nose pliers to press the cut end firmly against the clasp.

9 Use a 2" (5cm) length of stringing wire to string a pearl bead to the beginning of the necklace. Use the excess wire and another crimp bead to attach the flower clasp. Trim the excess wires.

Repeat for the other end of the necklace, using a 2" (5cm) piece of stringing wire to first attach 3 stone chips and then the hook portion.

THREE PEAS IN A POD

There's no question that I often have trouble keeping my peas in a pod. My three children have me running all over the place! This is a case where jewelry making is so much easier than parenting—a little jeweler's hammering and wrapping is all it takes to keep each set of three beads in place. The pod frame is a snap to make, so you might consider sharing these tidy earrings with friends and family.

MATERIALS

20-gauge half-hard sterling silver wire

24-gauge half-hard sterling silver wire

6 8mm round green raku beads (Blue Moon Beads)

TOOLS

ring mandrel

round-nose pliers

chain-nose pliers

flush cutters

jeweler's hammer

bench block

sanding stick

Finished dangle length: 2" (5cm)

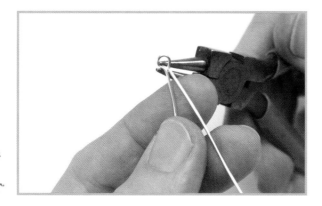

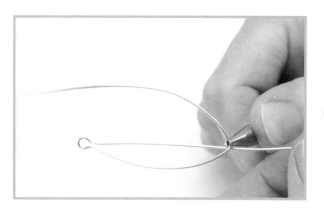

1 Working directly from the spool of 20-gauge wire, create a hanging loop by wrapping the wire around the round-nose pliers 2¼" (5.5cm) from the wire end at the base of the loop.

2 Use your fingertips to curve the wire (use the wire end that is still attached to the spool). Pinch the wire with chain-nose pliers 1½" (4cm) from the base of the loop. Bend the wire back up and shape it to make the other half of the pod.

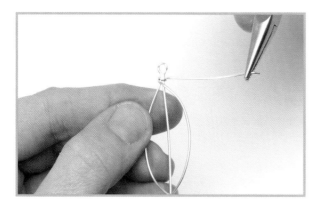

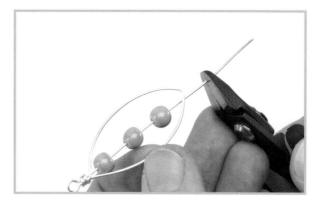

3 Using the flush cutters, cut the wire from the spool, leaving a 1½" (4cm) tail. Grip the wire tail with the chain-nose pliers and wrap the wire around the base of the loop 2 times. Trim the wire end. Use the chain-nose pliers to press the cut wire against the base of the loop.

4 String 3 beads onto the center wire. Trim the wire ¼" (6mm) below the base of the pod.

5 Lifting the pod frame out of the way, hammer the ¾" (2cm) tip of the center wire on the bench block.

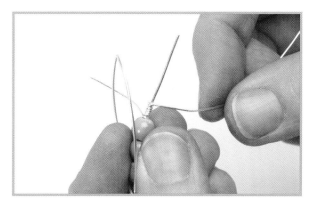

6 Wrap a 4" (10cm) section of 24-gauge wire 6 times above the ¾" (2cm) hammered portion of wire to hold the beads in place.

Repeat steps 1–6 to make an identical dangle.

7 Create 2 earwires with the 20-gauge wire (see Making Earwires on page 13). Hook one earwire to the loop at the top of each dangle.

SUSPENDED CORAL EARRINGS

I t's incredibly easy to bend wire into a rectangular frame; adding beads to the frame takes just a little wire wrapping. I intentionally selected irregular center drilled coral beads to break the predictability of the frame. The juxtaposition makes the finished earrings more interesting. If you have trouble finding the coral beads, a series of round disk beads should have the same contrasting effect.

MATERIALS

20-gauge half-hard
     sterling silver wire
24-gauge half-hard
     sterling silver wire
8 4mm × 10mm red tube
     coral beads

TOOLS

ring mandrel
round-nose pliers
chain-nose pliers
bent-nose pliers
flush cutters
jeweler's hammer
bench block
sanding stick
Finished dangle length:
     1¾" (4.5cm)

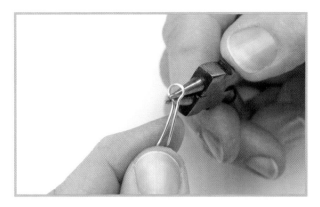

1 Working off the spool of 20-gauge sterling silver wire, create a hanging loop by wrapping the wire around the round-nose pliers ¼" (6mm) from the wire end. Use the pliers to bend the wire tails out at the base of the loop.

2 After ¼" (6mm) of straight wire, use the chain-nose pliers to bend the wire down to form the top left corner of the rectangle. Bend it again after 1¾" (4.5cm) to form the bottom left corner, and again after ½" (1.5cm) to make the bottom right corner. Make a final bend after 1¾" (4.5cm) to make the top right corner.

3 Using the flush cutters, trim the wire off the spool, leaving a 2" (5cm) tail. Wrap the wire end around the base of the loop ½" (1.5cm) from the top right corner. After 3 wraps, trim both wire ends with the flush cutters.

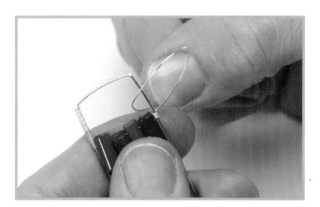

4 Cut an 8" (20.5cm) piece of 24-gauge wire. String 4 coral beads onto the center of the wire. Position the beads across the bottom third of the rectangle. Begin wrapping the wire ends around either side of the rectangle frame. Compress the wrapped wire (see Compressing a Coil on page 15). Continue wrapping down the side until the wraps measure ½" (1.5cm). Trim the wires.

Repeat steps 1–4 to make a second dangle.

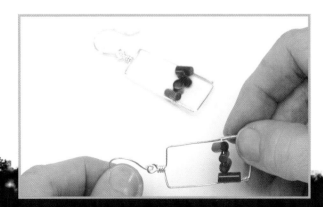

5 Create 2 earwires (see Making Earwires on page 13) with the 20-gauge wire. Attach earwires to the hanging loop of the finished dangles.

Chapter 2

TWISTED AND LINKED

Being well connected is vitally important in (life and) wire jewelry making. Wire links come in all shapes and sizes, and each has its own merits. The more you explore the linking techniques in this chapter, the larger the repertoire you'll have to draw from when creating your own designs.

The most basic link is the humble jump ring, but even it can be elevated when multiplied. Groups of four heavyweight copper jump rings connect to make the sturdy *Copper Link Bracelet* (page 53). With the addition of rubber O-rings, plain wire jump rings become an integral part of the *Stretch Rubber O-Ring Bracelet* (page 61). But jump rings don't have to do all the work. In the *Twisted Aluminum Bracelet* (page 50), large twisted aluminum jump rings are purely decorative, adding visual heft with very little weight.

Beaded links take several steps to create, but after you've mastered one, you'll be able to quickly repeat the steps to make additional links. Before your very eyes, a sparkling chain will grow, and your necklace will take shape. The small hammered and turned links in the *Jig Link Necklace* (page 57) take on the appearance of a rustic rosary chain. The strength of the wire ensures the simple turned loops will hold their shape. The wire used in the *Antique Brass Wrapped Links Necklace* (page 64) is finer, and each link is wrapped to increase its strength so the finished strand can withstand more wear.

The *Flight of Fancy Necklace* (page 69) showcases the most complex link in this chapter. Despite the wire bends, twists and loops, the fanciful flying-bird shape is still a link. The bird's beaks hook around the tail of the bird before it. From jump rings to birds and beyond, start exploring the countless ways to twist and link pieces of wire into stunning jewelry.

TWISTED ALUMINUM BRACELET

Aluminum wire carries huge visual weight but has the advantage of being featherlight to craft with and wear. With the help of the wire twister, three strands of 18-gauge wire easily twist and coil to form decorative jump rings. Even the 12-gauge wire is deceptively flexible; it coils into bulky jump rings and creates the knotted toggle portion of the clasp. The scale of the aluminum wire components perfectly balances the large stone beads. The result is a statement bracelet that is comfortable to wear.

MATERIALS

12-gauge silver aluminum wire

10" (25.5cm) length of .024

18-gauge silver aluminum wire (use a new spool)

49-strand silver stringing wire

2 size-3 silver crimp beads

4 11mm × 8mm corrugated silver metal beads

2 16mm × 10mm corrugated silver metal beads

3 14mm round dyed semiprecious stone beads

2 20mm turquoise-colored disk beads

1 30mm × 20mm oval red-dyed fire agate stone bead

8 silver bead caps

TOOLS

wire twister

jump ring maker with 8mm mandrel

ring mandrel

chain-nose pliers

bent-nose pliers

flush cutters

jeweler's hammer

bench block

Finished length: 8½" (21.5cm)

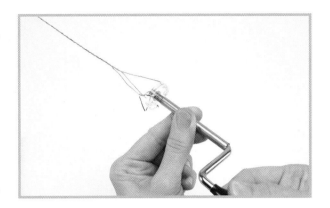

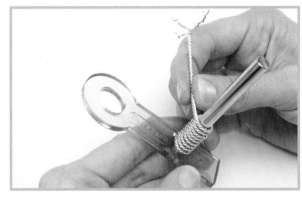

1   Divide the spool of 18-gauge wire into 3 separate pieces of wire of equal length. Twist one end of each wire piece through the holes in the wire twister. Bring the opposite ends of the wires together and anchor the ends around a stable post (I used a doorknob). Stand away from the post so the wires are straightened. Wind the handle until all 3 wires are evenly twisted.

2   Remove the twisted wire from the stable post and the wire twister. Coil the twisted wire 12 times up the jump ring maker and cut the coils apart to make 11 twisted jump rings (see Making Jump Rings on page 14). Coil the 12-gauge aluminum 12 times up the mandrel to make 11 plain jump rings

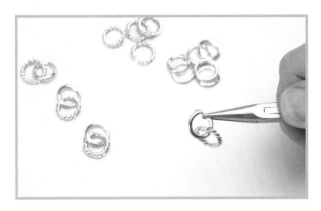

3   Link a twisted jump ring to each plain jump ring (see Opening and Closing Jump Rings on page 15).

4   Wrap the remaining twisted wire around the mandrel to make an 18mm (⅝" [1.6cm] on the mandrel) O-ring for the clasp.

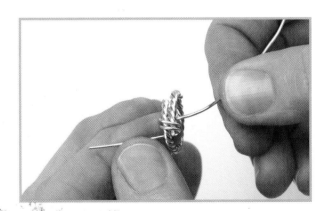

5   Slide the ring off the mandrel and wrap a single thickness of 18-gauge wire 4 times around the overlapping wires to hold them in place. Trim away all excess wires and use your chain-nose pliers to squeeze any loose ends flat against the ring.

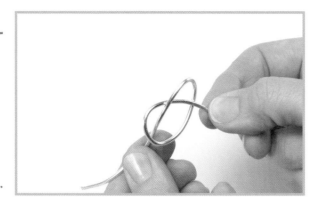

6 Tie a 6" (15cm) piece of 12-gauge wire into a knot to make the clasp toggle.

7 Gently pull the ends to tighten the knot until it is the right size. Trim the ends so they're ½" (1.5cm) long; the toggle should fit easily in and out of the O-ring. Hammer the ends on the bench block with the planishing side of the jeweler's hammer.

8 Cut a 10" (25.5cm) length of the 49-strand silver stringing wire. Crimp one end of the stringing wire to the knot portion of the toggle clasp (see Crimping Stringing Wire on page 18).

String the following sequence onto the wire: small corrugated bead, twisted ring (linked with plain ring), bead cap, round stone bead, bead cap, plain ring (linked with twisted ring), small corrugated bead, twisted ring (linked with plain ring), turquoise disk, plain ring (linked with twisted ring), large corrugated bead, twisted ring (linked with plain ring), bead cap, round stone bead, bead cap, plain ring (linked with twisted ring), small corrugated bead, twisted ring (linked with plain ring), bead cap, oval stone, bead cap, plain ring (linked with twisted ring), large corrugated bead, plain ring (linked with twisted ring), turquoise disk, twisted ring (plain ring), bead cap, round stone bead, bead cap, plain ring (linked with twisted ring), small corrugated bead.

9 String a crimp bead onto the stringing wire and loop the wire between the 4 wire wraps on the O-ring. Thread the wire end back down through the crimp bead and a corrugated bead. Pull the stringing wire tight before squeezing the crimp bead flat. Trim away the excess wire.

COPPER LINK BRACELET

This earthy bracelet is made with copper from the hardware store. Unlike its nontarnish counterparts sold in craft and jewelry stores, hardware-store copper wire quickly takes on an aged appearance; a wipe of the jewelry cloth will instantly bring back shiny copper. I like how the natural tarnishing integrates with the charms and stones, but you could easily make a low-maintenance version by substituting with nontarnish copper. The construction is a basic chain maille technique with a little decorative wrapping to attach the stone bead dangles.

MATERIALS

18-gauge copper wire

24-gauge copper wire

3 top-drilled polished stone beads

turtle charm

TOOLS

jump ring maker with 6mm, 9mm and 14mm mandrels

round-nose pliers

chain-nose pliers

bent-nose pliers

round-nose pliers

flush cutters

Finished length: 7½" (19cm)

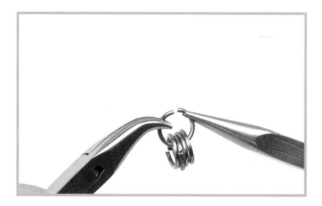

1 Make 113 9mm jump rings using the 18-gauge copper wire (see Making Jump Rings on page 14). It takes 4 jump rings to make each link on the bracelet. String 1 open ring through 4 closed rings and then close it (see Opening and Closing Jump Rings on page 15).

2 Link three more jump rings through the closed rings. You should have two groups of four jump rings linked together. String 1 open ring through the second set of 4 closed rings and then close it.

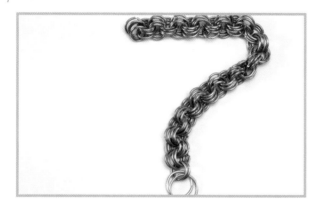

3 Repeat steps 1–2 until 27 sets of four links are used and the bracelet measures 6¼" (16cm). Use 18-gauge wire to make two 14mm rings. Use two 9mm rings to link two 14mm to the end of the bracelet for the O-ring clasp. Add the two 9mm jump rings through the last set of 4 jump rings on the opposite end.

4 Cut approximately 16" (40.5cm) of 24-gauge wire. Thread a stone bead onto the center of the wire and then coil each end of the wire around an O-ring. It may be helpful to use the bent-nose pliers to tightly wrap the wire ends. Repeat this step for the remaining O-ring.

5 Cut a 4" (10cm) piece of 18-gauge wire to make a hook clasp (see Making Hook and O-Ring Clasps on page 19). Use two 9mm jump rings to attach the clasp to the other end of the bracelet.

6 Use 18-gauge wire to make three 6mm rings. Link a charm to the 2 finished O-rings. Repeat the wrapping technique from step 4 on the final 9mm jump ring, adding the final stone bead. Use the three 6mm links to attach the wrapped 9mm ring to the O-ring clasp.

FLOWER EARRINGS

There's nothing like hanging a pair of posies from my ears to put me in a sunny mood at the start of the day. With one continuous piece of wire, you'll make petals, a leaf and the earring finding. I like the pop of orange, but you can use any color bead to accent these graphic earrings.

MATERIALS

20-gauge German-style silver-plated wire (Beadalon)

1 3mm round red coral bead

Aleene's Jewelry & Metal Glue

TOOLS

round-nose pliers

chain-nose pliers

flush cutters

jeweler's hammer

bench block

sanding stick

Finished length: 2" (5cm)

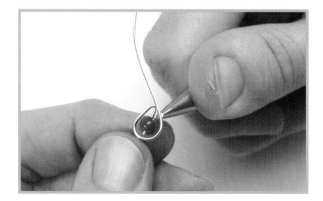

1 Working directly from the spool of 20-gauge wire, poke the wire end into a red coral bead. Bend the wire down ⅛" (3mm) from the top of the bead. Wrap the wire around the bead to encircle it.

2 Pinch the wire with the round-nose pliers to bend it up at a 90-degree angle (this will form the base of the first petal). Shape the wire around the round-nose pliers ½" (1.5cm) from the petal base to form the top of the petal. Create another fold ½" (1.5cm) down from the petal to form the base of the next petal. Repeat this step to create a total of 6 petals.

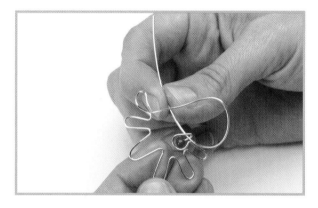

3 Pull 4" (10cm) of wire from the spool and use the flush cutters to cut it from the spool. Thread the wire end through the ⅛" (3mm) wire loop at the top of the bead. Pull the wire through and arrange the bent wire petals around the bead center.

4 Leave ½" (1.5cm) of straight wire stem before twisting a ½" (1.5cm) long leaf. Place the finished flower and leaf over the bench block and hammer it with the ball end of the hammer to dimple the wire. Avoid hitting the bead and the twisted wires.

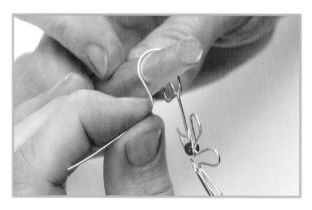

5 Form the end of the wire into an earwire (see Making Earwires on page 13). Trim the excess wire as needed.

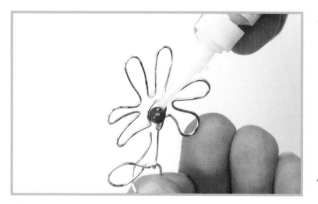

6 Squeeze a tiny amount of glue into the bead to ensure it stays connected to the wire end.

Repeat steps 1–6 to make a second earring, facing the leaf in the opposite direction. Allow the glue to dry thoroughly before wearing the earrings.

JIG LINK NECKLACE

When it comes to wire work, the jig is not a dance but a metal board with pegs that helps you make consistent ornate links. It's quick and easy to form a custom design after arranging the metal pegs on the board. I used a series of simple beaded and hammered links to connect the ornate links and infuse color into the necklace design.

MATERIALS

22-gauge nickel wire

5 6mm jump rings made with 20-gauge nickel wire (see page 14)

5 teardrop-shaped glass beads

1 8mm round red glass bead

26 4mm–6mm assorted round, bicone and square glass beads (turquoise, pink, red, black, light green)

1 long green glass bead

TOOLS

jig board, pegs and plastic sleeves

chain-nose pliers

round-nose pliers

flush cutters

jeweler's hammer

bench block

Finished length: 16½" (42cm)

A NOTE ABOUT NICKEL ALLERGY

I intentionally used the darker, less shiny nickel for this project. If you have a nickel allergy, replace the nickel wire with another wire in the same gauge (one exception: Avoid aluminum—it's not strong enough for this technique).

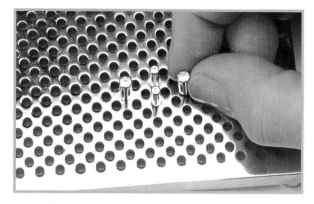

1 Position the wider pegs 2 holes apart on the jig board. Place 2 small pegs between the large pegs.

2 Anchor all 4 pegs by threading plastic sleeves onto the underside of the pegs.

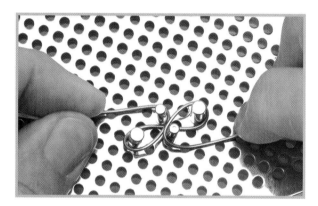

3 Working from the spool, wrap the wire around one large peg and then the second large peg. Wrap the wire ends around the small pegs. Lift the shaped wire off the jig board.

4 Trim the wire and use the chain-nose pliers to tighten the looped ends. Hammer the finished link to harden the wire. Repeat steps 3–4 to make 3 more links, for a total of 4 links.

5 Cut a ¾" (2cm) section of wire to make a beaded link. String a glass bead onto the center of the wire. Hammer both ends of the wire on the bench block to flatten the metal.

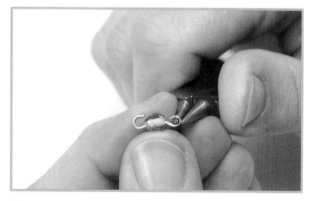

6 Use the round-nose pliers to turn the flattened wire ends into loops. Repeat steps 5–6 to make a total of 26 beaded links.

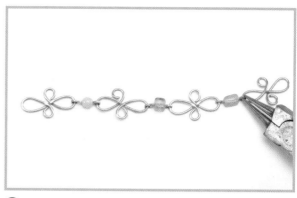

7 Hook 11 beaded links together to make one side of the necklace and 12 links together to make the other side of the necklace.

8 Use the 3 remaining beaded links to connect the 4 jig links.

9 Connect the beaded links to either side of the jig link section.

10 To make the ornate ring portion of the clasp, position 4 large pegs in a square formation on the pegboard. Make sure each peg is spaced 1 hole apart. Using 2 small pegs, position 1 in a hole above the square and the other in a hole below. Anchor the pegs with plastic sleeves.

Working from the spool, thread the large red bead onto the wire and position it in the center of the peg square. Wrap the free wire end around the 2 pegs at the top of the square; finish by looping it around the small top peg. Wrap the bottom wire end around the 2 large pegs at the bottom of the square; finish by looping it around the small bottom peg.

11 Slide the bent wire off the jig board. Trim the excess wire and use the chain-nose pliers to close the loops. Hammer the clasp on the bench block to harden the wire.

12 Connect the ornate ring to the twelfth beaded link. Repeat steps 5–6 using the long glass bead on a longer wire section. Attach the long glass bead dangle onto the end of the ornate ring.

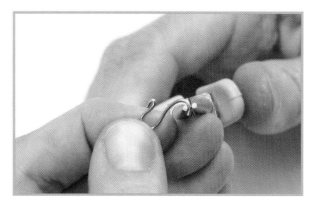

13 Form a small hook clasp with a 1½" (4cm) length of wire. Hammer it to harden the metal. Connect the finished hook to the eleventh beaded link on the other side of the necklace.

14 Use the jump rings to hang a teardrop at the bottom of each bent link and at the end of the long beaded link.

STRETCH RUBBER O-RING BRACELET

For all it's amazing attributes, wire is unyielding in the flexibility department, which makes stretchy rubber O-rings the perfect component to pair with wire. By linking folded rubber O-rings through sturdy 12- and 16-gauge wire jump rings, you'll create a bracelet both strong and flexible. The potential for exciting color combinations is endless because both the rubber O-rings and the wires come in multiple hues. The purple and red in this design are mirrored in the stunning glass heart dangle made by Cathi Milligan of Beadbrains.

MATERIALS

12-gauge purple aluminum wire

16-gauge red aluminum wire

48 10mm red rubber O-rings (The Ring Lord)

heart-shaped bead (Beadbrains by Cathi Milligan)

TOOLS

jump ring maker with 6mm and 12mm mandrels

flush cutter

round-nose pliers

chain-nose pliers

bent-nose pliers

flush cutters

Finished length: 8½" (21.5cm)

1 Create twelve 12mm purple jump rings using the 12-gauge wire and the jump ring maker (see Making Jump Rings on page 14). Make twenty-six 6mm red jump rings using the 16-gauge wire.

Slide a rubber O-ring into a red jump ring.

2 Add a second rubber O-ring into the jump ring. Position the O-rings so an even amount of rubber extends out either side of the metal ring. If needed, use the bent-nose pliers to make adjustments. Close the jump ring (see Opening and Closing Jump Rings on page 15).

Repeat the second half of step 1 and all of step 2 to make 23 double-stuffed red jump rings, for a total of 24.

3 Use the purple jump rings to link the rubber-stuffed O-rings into a bracelet. Slide one end of the purple wire through the top and bottom of a single O-ring.

4 Repeat step 3 to connect a total of 4 O-rings to the purple jump ring. Carefully close the ring. Two of the rubber rings will situate themselves on each side of the purple ring.

5 Slide a purple jump ring through the top and bottom of the 2 suspended O-rings on one side of the first jump ring.

6 Thread 2 new connected rubber O-rings onto the other side of the purple ring. Close the purple ring.

7 Repeat steps 5–6 until you've used all the double-stuffed O-rings. Finish by connecting the second half of the last (twelfth) purple jump ring to the remaining 2 suspended O-rings from the first purple jump ring.

8 Cut a 3" (7.5cm) section of red wire. Form a small loop at the end of the wire with the round-nose pliers. String the heart bead onto the wire. Form a hanging loop at the top of the bead.

9 Hook the heart bead onto a purple jump ring.

ANTIQUE BRASS WRAPPED LINKS NECKLACE

There's nothing like the rich colors and texture of Vintaj charms, beads and wire to get your creative juices flowing. The wrapped, beaded link construction creates a sturdy necklace that can withstand regular wear. What makes this design unique is that the ornate closure is also the focal point of the necklace. What keeps the necklace intriguing is the variety of bead shapes, the sparkling faceted beads, the ornate bead caps and the bird charm.

MATERIALS

18-gauge nontarnish bronze wire (Vintaj)
20-gauge nontarnish bronze wire (Vintaj)
24-gauge nontarnish bronze wire (Vintaj)
6 5mm 20-gauge jump rings (see page 14)
3 16mm faceted aqua glass beads
3 12mm × 6mm opalescent rectangle glass beads
2 16mm × 20mm faceted green rectangle glass beads
1 10mm faceted green bicone glass bead
2 10mm purple flower glass beads
2 12mm × 8mm faceted topaz oval glass beads
2 8mm faceted yellow glass beads
1 8mm green rondelle glass bead (for dangle)
3 pink disk, round and oval-shaped glass beads
3 assorted-sized turquoise bicone glass beads
2 beige round glass beads
2 beige teardrop-shaped glass beads (reserve 1 for dangle)
2 center-drilled purple disk glass beads
1 center-drilled brown disk glass bead
1 3mm turquoise round glass bead (for dangle)
1 lentil-shaped lampwork bead (Vintaj)
3 brass bead caps (Vintaj)
1 brass bird charm (Vintaj)

TOOLS

ring mandrel
jump ring maker with 6mm mandrel
round-nose pliers
chain-nose pliers
flush cutters
jeweler's hammer
bench block

Finished length: 24" (61cm) plus 3" (6.5cm) dangle

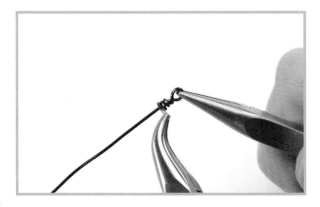

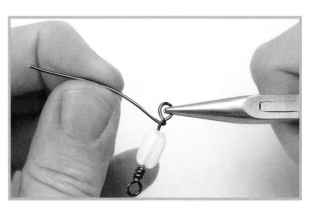

1 Cut a 4" (10cm) length of 20-gauge wire. Beginning ½" (1.5cm) from the end, form a loop around your round-nose pliers. Trap the loop in the chain-nose pliers while you wrap the wire 3 times around the base. Trim the wrapped wire end.

2 Thread one of the glass beads onto the other wire end, and wrap the wire ¼" (6mm) from where it emerges from the bead around your round-nose pliers to form a second loop. Wrap the wire end 3 times around the base of the loop before trimming the wire.

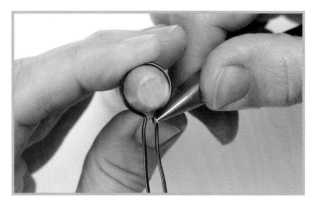

3 Repeat steps 1–2 to begin making your second beaded loop; this time, before wrapping the second loop closed, link it through a loop on your first link. Continue working in this fashion, adding 24 more new links to your chain (for a total of 26). Be conscious of spreading the varieties and colors of glass beads throughout the chain. Be sure to leave the 3mm turquoise bead, turquoise bicone, teardrop beige and green rondelle beads for the dangle.

4 Wrap a 7" (18cm) section of 18-gauge wire around the end of the ring mandrel to make a ½" (1.5cm) diameter O-ring. Using the chain-nose pliers, bend the wire tails so they hang down.

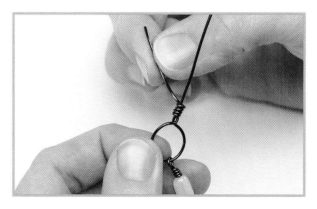

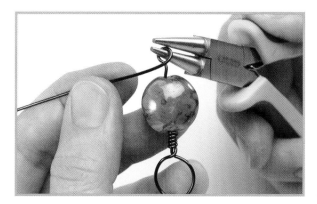

5 Slide the O-ring off the mandrel. Thread the O-ring through the last link of the beaded chain. Grasp the O-ring with your fingers (or trap it in the chain-nose pliers) and wrap one of the wire tails 4 times around the other at the base of the O-ring to secure it. Trim the excess wrapping wire, leaving an open wrapped wire tail.

6 String the lentil bead onto the open wire tail. Leave ⅛" (3mm) of straight wire before shaping it around the jump ring maker or round-nose pliers to make a 6mm connector loop. Wrap the wire 3 times around the base of the loop to secure the bead.

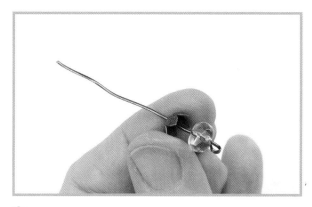

7 Tightly wrap 24-gauge wire around the entire O-ring. Pass the wire through the link to complete wrapping the other side of the ring. When you have wrapped the entire ring, trim the excess wire and press the cut ends into the wraps with the chain-nose pliers.

8 To create the flower-bud dangle, cut a 2" (5cm) length of 20-gauge wire and pound one end of it flat. Curl the flattened end up into a loop with the tip of the round-nose pliers. Slide the green rondelle bead and a petal bead cap onto the wire.

9 Shape the wire ⅛" (3mm) from where it emerges from the bead cap into a loop. Link the loop to the O-ring connector loop before wrapping it closed.

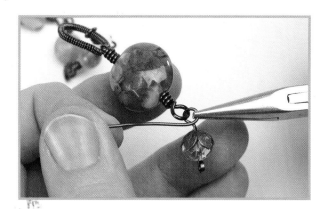

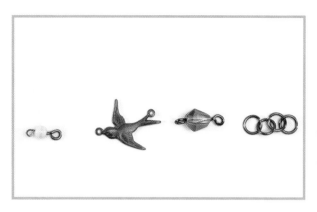

10 Make a second flower-bud dangle with a 3" (7.5cm) length of wire and the beige teardrop bead. Do not link it to the O-ring before wrapping its loop closed. Instead use 2 jump rings to connect it alongside the first bud.

11 The longest dangle begins with the 3mm turquoise round bead strung onto a 1" (2.5cm) length of 18-gauge wire that has been hammered and curled. Link the other end of the wire to the bird charm. Hook the other end of the bird to a 1" (2.5cm) link with a turquoise bead.

12 Four jump rings link the connected beaded link to the O-ring.

13 Create a 1¼" (3cm) long open spiral hook with the 18-gauge wire (see Making a Spiral on page 16). Form the other end into a 6mm loop. Hammer both the spiral and the loop to harden the wire.

14 Link the loop to the last link of the necklace before wrapping and trimming the end.

FLIGHT OF FANCY NECKLACE

This project evolved by trial and error, and you would probably laugh if you could see the series of failed bird attempts. I was ecstatic when the finished bird pattern took shape. It meets all my requirements: It uses easy-to-manipulate 20-gauge wire, it can be quickly duplicated and it can be linked to form a continuous chain. It might take you a couple attempts to get your hands used to the process, but the finished necklace is worth the effort.

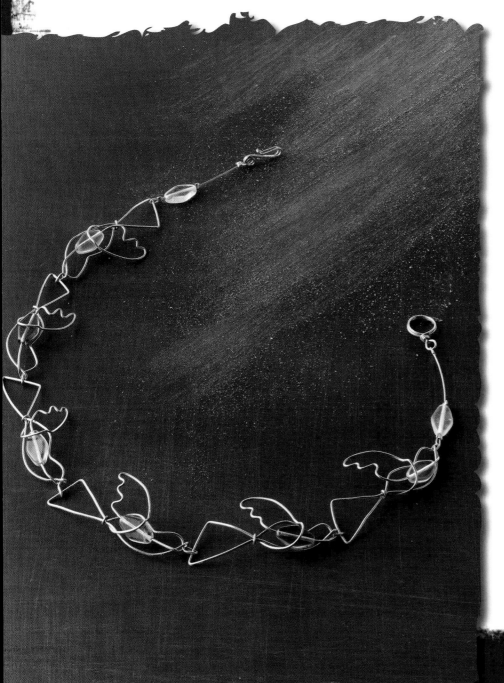

MATERIALS

20-gauge silver-colored wire

.024 silver-colored stringing wire

8 diamond-shaped glass beads in blue, clear, yellow and shades of green

6 size No. 1 crimp beads

TOOLS

round-nose pliers

chain-nose pliers

flush cutters

Finished length: 17" (43cm)

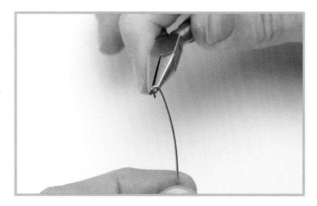

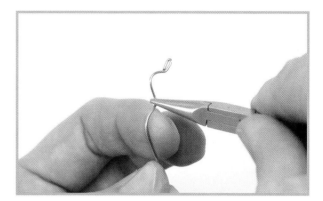

1 Cut a 13" (33cm) length of 20-gauge wire. Use the chain-nose pliers to fold the end back ¼" (6cm) to make the beak.

2 Use the chain-nose pliers to grab the wire at the base of the beak, bending it up to start shaping the head. Use your fingertips to shape a rounded head that's ⅓" (8mm) long. Grab the wire with the pliers to create a bend at the base of the neck. Use your fingertips to create a rounded back that is ½" (1.5cm) long.

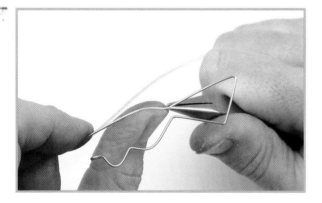

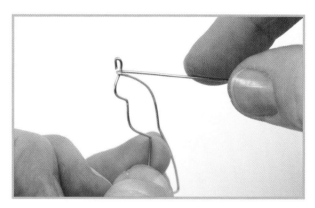

3 Grab the wire at the end of the body to create a fold at the base of the tail. Use the round-nose pliers to create a fold in the top of the tail ⅓" (8mm) from the base of the tail. Create a second fold ¼" (6mm) from the top of the tail to mark the end of the tail. Pinch the wire 1" (2.5cm) from the last bend to form the bottom of the tail base.

4 Use your fingertips to shape the wire into a rounded belly. Wrap the wire up and around the beak; be careful not to pull the wire tight, or you may distort the bird's belly.

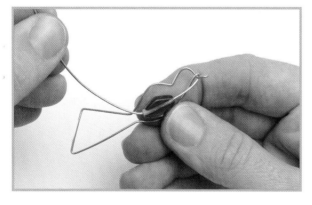

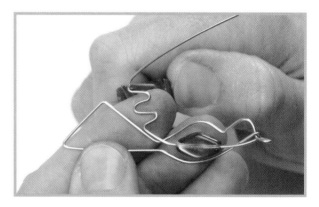

5 Bring the wire across the front of the bird. String a bead onto the wire, and position it in the middle of the bird's body.

6 Lift the wire up toward the bird's back and then use the round-nose pliers to form 3 rounded wing tips.

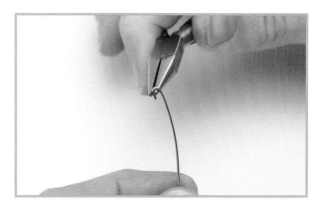

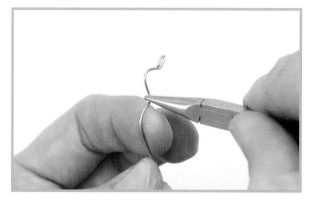

7 Use your fingertips to curve the wire toward the bird's head and belly to create the front part of the wing. Wrap the wire around the 2 wires at the base of the tail. Trim away any excess wire.

Repeat steps 1–7 to make 5 more birds, alternating the color of the body bead.

8 Arrange the 6 birds on your work surface, positioning your favorite birds in the center of the necklace. Working with 2 birds at a time, use the round-nose pliers to carefully open the beak of 1 bird and then link it around the end of the next bird tail. Make sure the wire beak is tightly closed.

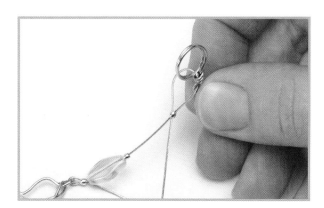

9 Make a double hook and O-ring clasp with 20-gauge wire (see Making Hook and O-Ring Clasps on page 19). Cut two 3" (8cm) lengths of the stringing wire. Crimp the stringing wire through the first bird's beak (see Crimping Stringing Wire on page 18). String a bead onto the wire. String a second crimp bead onto the wire and squeeze it alongside the last bead to hold the crimp bead in position. Leave 1" (2.5cm) of exposed stringing wire before crimping the O-ring clasp to the end of the wire.

Repeat step 9 to attach the second stringing wire, bead and hook portion of the clasp to the end of the last bird's tail.

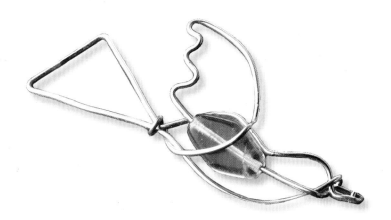

DOUBLE LOOP EARRINGS

I absolutely love the simplicity of these earrings: They're lightweight and elegant—perfect everyday wear. The success of this design hinges on the thick, silver-plated stringing wire; it has the flexibility and strength to make resilient loops. I chose these faceted Amazonite beads because the neutral color works well with lots of outfits, but you can use any pair of natural stone beads as long as the hole can accommodate the center wire.

MATERIALS

22-gauge German-style silver-plated wire (Beadalon)

2 5" (13cm) lengths of 24-gauge German-style silver-plated wire (Beadalon)

.30 49-strand silver-plated stringing wire

2 faceted Amazonite stone beads

TOOLS

ring mandrel
round-nose pliers
chain-nose pliers
flush cutters
jeweler's hammer
bench block
sanding stick

Finished dangle length: 1⅝" (4cm)

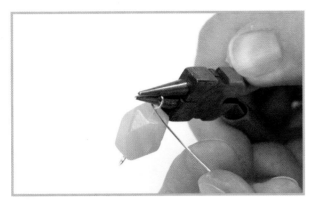

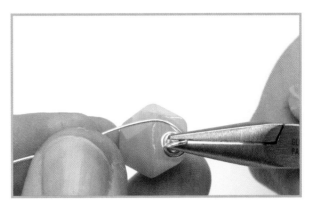

1 Working from the spool of 22-gauge wire, pass the wire through a bead. Form a loop on both sides with the round-nose pliers. Wrap the wire around the base of the loops to secure it.

2 Make additional wraps to create a decorative wire spiral before trimming the wire.

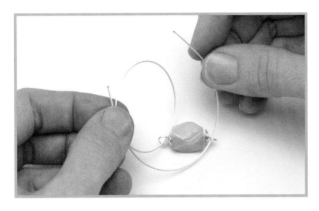

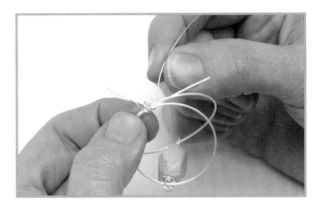

3 Cut two 11" (28cm) lengths of the stringing wire. Pass the stringing wire through a loop on one side of the stone. Form the wire into a circle before stringing the end through the other side of the stone.

4 Pinch the 2 wire ends and center of the 2 circles between your fingertip. Pull or tighten any slack from either end. If necessary, make adjustments until you have 2 even 1¼" (3cm) diameter circles with the stone falling in the center between them. Wrap the 5" (13cm) length of 24-gauge wire 4 times around all 3 wires to hold them in place.

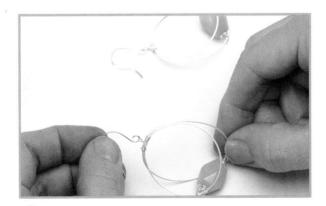

5 Use the round-nose pliers to form a hanging loop and then make 4 more wraps before trimming the wire and stringing the wire ends. Use the chain-nose pliers to push the wire ends flat against the stringing wire.

Repeat steps 1–5 to make a second earring.

Create earwires (see Making Earwires on page 13) and link an earwire to the hanging loop on each earring.

Chapter 3

KNITTED AND STITCHED

Wire is a versatile material that can lend itself to many techniques. As a testament to its versatility, wire can easily replace yarn and thread to be knitted, stitched and so much more. In this chapter, you'll learn how to create wire accents to complement beads or make the wire the main focus, all while learning basic techniques from crafts usually reserved for fiber enthusiasts.

This chapter runs the gamut of fiber-to-wire pieces. You'll string felt balls onto memory wire to make the soft *Felt Bead Bracelet* (page 90), and use a child's knitting spool to create the comfortable and flexible *Knitted Stretch Bracelet* (page 80). The easy, freeform technique in the *Bird's Nest Pendant* (page 86) makes a beautiful focus for a wooden pendant. Try your hand at knotting the *Macramé Bracelet* (page 83) or crocheting a beaded necklace (page 76). For a final challenge, grab a hook and crochet a pair of colorful *Crocheted Circle Earrings* (page 93).

At first glance, you might dismiss these designs as being complicated, but give them a closer look. In every case, there's a simple stitch technique that is broken down into easy-to-follow steps. Making jewelry with these methods relies heavily on thinner (higher) gauges of wire that are flexible enough to easily form multiple loops, so repeating these steps builds the piece, giving thin wires strength, form and functionality.

After exploring these techniques, you might start looking more closely at accessories in your home and wardrobe; I guarantee you'll discover the very same stitches.

CROCHETED NECKLACE

This single crochet stitch makes an elegant beaded strand—the perfect do-it-yourself alternative to a purchased chain. The beads are strung onto the wire at the beginning and easily slide into place between each stitch. You can decrease the gauge of wire to make a thicker strand and increase the size of the needle to form larger loops. If you select larger beads, you can forgo the pendant and make an attractive necklace of crochet strands.

MATERIALS

18-gauge silver-colored wire

3 6mm 18-gauge silver-colored wire jump rings (see page 14)

28-gauge silver-colored wire (see page 14)

1 10mm 18-gauge silver-colored wire jump ring

1 strand 6mm round iridescent green beads

1 strand 4mm round red cat's-eye beads

1 strand 4mm round brown glass pearls

1 strand 4mm round pink faceted glass beads

green glass pendant (Plaid)

TOOLS

metal-tipped size D 3.0mm crochet hook (Clover)

jump ring mandrel

chain-nose pliers

round-nose pliers

flush cutters

Finished length: approximately 18" (46cm)

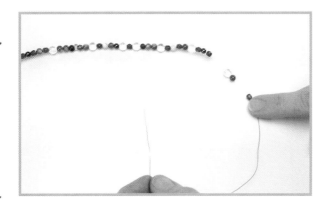

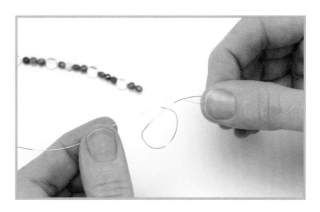

1 Randomly string approximately 56 round beads onto the 28-gauge wire. Don't cut the wire; you'll crochet directly from the spool.

2 Beginning 2" (5cm) from the end of the wire, form the wire into a circle.

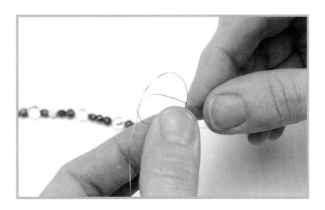

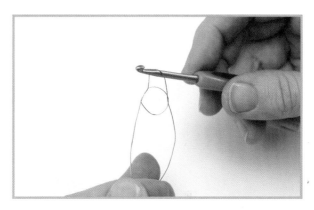

3 Bring the right hand-wire down behind the circle so it creates a line through the middle.

4 Use the crochet hook to pull the wire up through the center of the circle. The wire will form a small loop. You just completed the first chain stitch.

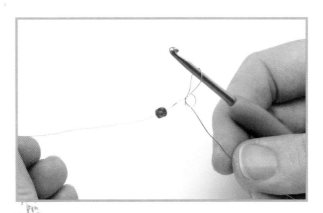

5 Slide a bead up the wire so it rests right beside the loop.

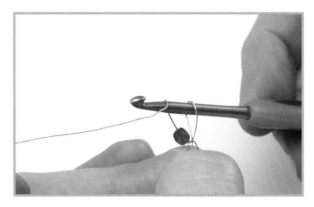

6   Wrap the wire once around the crochet hook.

7   Use the hook to pull this new wrapped loop through the first loop. The bead will be trapped in the new stitch.

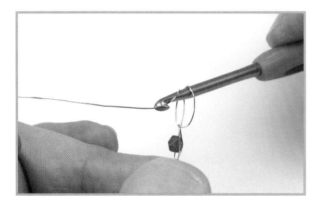

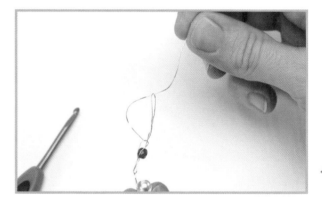

8   Repeat steps 6–7 to make the next stitch bead-free.

9   Repeat steps 5–8, crocheting the chain by alternating a beaded stitch with a plain wire stitch. The finished crochet wire should be twice the desired necklace length.

    Set the crochet needle aside. Using the flush cutters, cut the wire end and pull it through the last stitch.

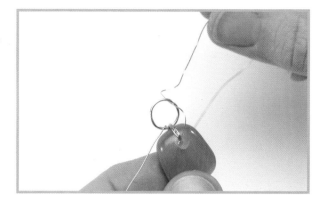

10 Cut a 12" (30.5cm) length of 28-gauge wire. String it through both the pendant hole and the 10mm jump ring. Repeat to wrap the pendant and jump ring together. Twist the ends of the wire to secure it. Use the wire cutters to trim any excess wire.

11 Fold the finished crochet wire in half to create a double strand. Use the chain-nose pliers to link the wired pendant to the center of the double strand with a 6mm jump ring (see Opening and Closing Jump Rings on page 15).

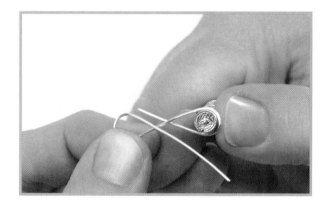

12 Cut a 6" (15cm) length of 18-gauge wire. Use a jump ring mandrel to form the wire into a figure eight.

13 Shape the ends with the round-nose pliers, trimming the wire as needed. Hammer the finished hook to strengthen it. This will be part of the clasp.

14 Link the 6mm jump rings to both ends of the double crochet chain. Hook the closed end of the hook to one of the rings before closing it.

KNITTED STRETCH BRACELET

Here's a new twist on your childhood knitting spool. Instead of wrapping the pegs with yarn, thread three strands of beaded stringing wire into the spool. With each new rotation, slide a bead into the center of the spool. The resulting beaded knitted cable is superstretchy and incredibly comfortable, making it perfect for everyday wear.

MATERIALS

.015 19-strand satin silver-colored stringing wire (Beadalon)

.015 19-strand silver-colored stringing wire (Beadalon)

.015 7-strand silver-colored stringing wire (Beadalon)

1 strand triangular natural shell beads

1 strand 11.5mm flat shell beads

1 strand 8mm × 12mm amber oval beads

1 strand ruby matte Czech glass beadettes

small tube silver seed beads

3 No. 1 silver crimp beads

TOOLS

knitting spool (Clover)

chain-nose pliers

flush cutters

Finished length: stretches to approximately 3½" (9cm), but you can make your bracelet larger by adding more beads or unbeaded stitches.

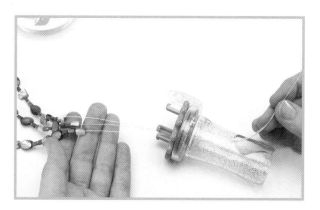

1 Working directly from all 3 spools of stringing wire, string each wire with 8" (20.5cm) of a random assortment of all the bead varieties.

2 Draw all 3 wire ends down through the base of the knitting spool. Anchor them with one hand.

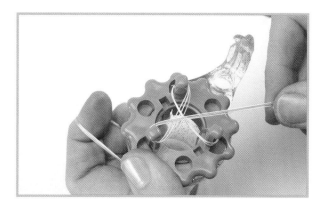

3 Follow the manufacturer's directions for looping the 3 threads around the top 3 spokes of the knitter.

4 Wrap the 3 strands around the spokes a second time. Grab the bottom 3 wire strands of the first rotation with the hook.

5 Lift them up and over the 3 strands of the last rotation and then let them fall into the center of the spool.

6 Slide 1 large bead or 1 beadette and seed bead from 1 of the strands. Repeat steps 4–5 to make another stitch.

7 Continue wrapping and lifting the bottom wires over each new wrap. Be sure to alternate which beads slide into the center of the spool before each new wire wrap. When the beaded section is long enough to comfortably fit around your wrist, pull it out through the top of the spool.

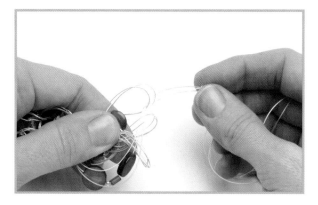

8 Cut the stringing wires from their spools, leaving at least 4" (10cm) of tail to make them easier to manipulate with. Unwrap the very end of the knitted piece.

9 Pair a strand from the beginning of the knitting with a strand from the end of the knitting. Thread the strands in opposite directions through a crimp bead and use the chain-nose pliers to squeeze the crimp flat. Repeat the process to crimp the remaining pairs of strands together. Trim any wire tails after securing them. The finished bracelet will have the appearance of a continuous circle.

MACRAMÉ BRACELET

Traditional macramé knots are made with hemp or bulky jute cord. The same basic knots, when made with cabled stringing wire, create elegant jewelry. Thin wire also makes it easy to add pearl, glass and faceted beads into your design. Instead of forcing the wire into a knotted closure, I took advantage of large crimp tubes and purchased clasps to finish the ends.

MATERIALS

.018 19-strand gold-colored stringing wire

5 10mm × 8mm brown glass beads

12 4mm round faceted brown glass beads

24 3mm freshwater pearls

2 antique gold crimp tubes

1 antique gold lobster clasp

TOOLS

chain-nose pliers

flush cutters

tape

Finished length: 7½" (19cm)

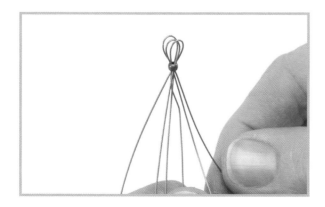

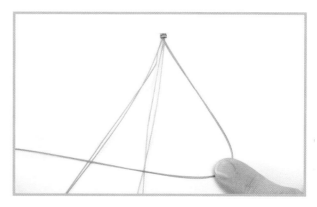

1 Cut three 1½ yard (1.5m) lengths of gold stringing wire. Fold the 3 lengths of stringing wire in half and then push the folds into a crimp tube. Continue pushing the wire until the folded ends make a ¼" (6mm) loop beyond the crimp. Use the chain-nose pliers to squeeze the crimp flat (see Crimping Stringing Wire on page 18).

2 Tape the loop of wires to the work surface. Separate the 6 wires into 3 pairs; the 2 outer wires on each side weave in and out, and the 2 center wires always keep their central position. Bring the right-hand wires across the center strands.

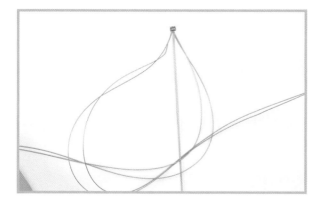

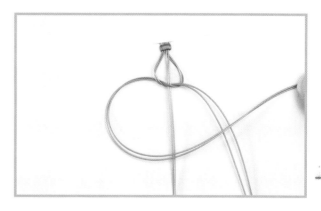

3 Bring the left-hand wires over the right, under the center wires and up through the bend in the right wire. Slide the knot up under the crimp. You've completed the first half of a square knot.

4 To finish the knot, bring the left-hand wires across the center wires.

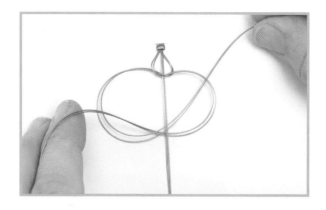

5 The right-hand wires now cross over the left, then go under the center and left wires, and finish by coming up through the bend in the left wires.

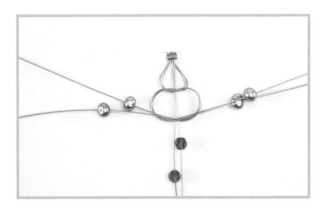

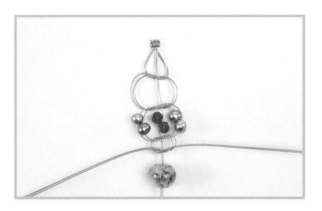

6 String the first bead sequence: 1 pearl onto each of the 4 outer wires, and 1 brown faceted bead on each of the center wires.

7 Repeat steps 2–5 to make a complete knot. String a single 10mm × 8mm brown glass bead onto both of the center strands. The outer wires remain unbeaded. Repeat steps 2–5 to make a complete knot.

8 Repeat steps 6–7 four times to string and knot the length of the bracelet. End by stringing the first bead sequence (step 6) one more time.

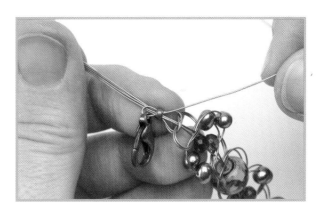

9 String all 6 wires into the other crimp tube and slide the crimp up against the last knot. String the clasp onto one wire end and then string it back through the crimp tube. Squeeze the crimp flat with the chain-nose pliers. Use the flush cutters to trim the 5 wire ends by the clasp and the single wire end by the knotted bracelet.

BIRD'S NEST PENDANT

ire is the perfect medium for nest building because it quickly spirals into this freeform shape. A second piece of wire stitches the finished nest and insets three pearl "eggs." I chose the wooden link as a natural perch for the finished nest; watching over the clutch of bead eggs is a modified bird charm. With so much detail in the pendant, I crimped three strands of cabled stringing wires to either side to form a simple necklace.

MATERIALS

22-gauge brass wire
22-gauge silver-colored wire
.015 gold-colored stringing wire (Beadalon)
3 pearl beads
wooden link (Blue Moon Beads)
bird charm (Plaid)
leaf charm
2 gold crimp tubes
1 gold lobster clasp
Aleene's Jewelry & Metal Glue

TOOLS

round-nose pliers
chain-nose pliers
flush cutter

Finished length: 20½" (52cm)

1 Spiral the 22-gauge brass wire into a 1" (2.5cm) wide circle, adding rotations to build up the sides of the nest.

2 Use the round-nose pliers to push the end of the wire down into the nest.

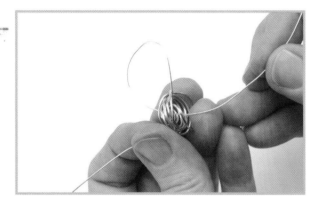

3 Push the silver wire end up through the base of the nest, wrap the wire around the outside of the nest and then bring the end back up through the base of the nest. Repeat this step to make 2 more evenly spaced stitches around the outside of the nest.

4 Bring the wire back up into the nest and string a pearl bead "egg" onto the wire. Bring the wire back down through the center of the nest.

5 Repeat step 4 two more times to nestle the remaining pearl bead eggs into the nest.
Use the round-nose pliers to grab and bend the brass wires around the nest to add texture.

6 Let the silver wire ends extend outside the base of the nest. Position the nest inside the wooden link. String the leaf charm onto one of the wires.

7   To attach the nest to the link, tightly wrap each silver wire around the wooden link 2 times. Twist the ends together and trim the excess wire with the flush cutters.

8   Use the flush cutters to trim the hanging loop off the top of the bird charm.

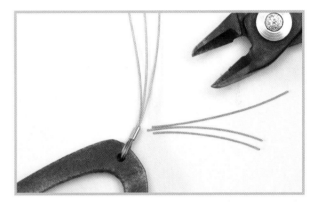

9   Position the bird to one side of the link. Glue the bird in place on the wooden link. Allow the glue to dry thoroughly before wearing.

10   Cut six 11" (28cm) lengths of the gold-colored stringing wire. Crimp 3 strands of stringing wire to the hole in one side of the wooden link (see Crimping Stringing Wire on page 18). Repeat this step to attach 3 strands to the other side of ' the link. Using the flush cutters, trim the 3 shorter tails of the wire, allowing the longer pieces to act as the chain.

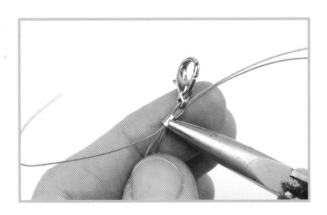

11   To add the clasp, string all 3 wires from one side into a crimp tube. String the clasp onto 1 wire end and then string it back through the crimp tube. Squeeze the crimp flat with the chain-nose pliers. Use flush cutters to trim the 2 wire ends by the clasp and the single wire end by the chain. Repeat this step to add the other half of the clasp to the other side of the necklace.

FELT BEAD BRACELET

The perfect marriage of opposites: soft wool felt balls and rigid memory wire. This project takes advantage of the stiff wire to string the felt balls, which encase the wire to form an extremely comfortable flexible bracelet. The felt balls come already beaded, but if you have trouble finding them, you can make your own by stitching seed beads onto the felt with a small sewing needle.

MATERIALS

3 rotations of bracelet memory wire (Remembrance by Beadalon)

20-gauge stainless steel wire

2 packages small warm-tone beaded felt balls (Dimensions)

1 package medium warm-tone beaded felt balls (Dimensions)

2 memory-wire bead caps

Aleene's Jewelry & Metal Glue

TOOLS

jump ring mandrel

chain-nose pliers

memory-wire cutters (regular cutting tool will be ruined by the memory wire)

flush cutters

jeweler's hammer

bench block

Finished diameter: 2½" (6.5cm)

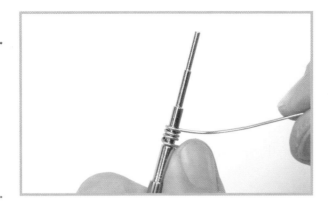

1 Cut a 4" (10cm) length of the 20-gauge wire with the flush cutters. Coil the wire 4 or 5 times around the 4mm section of the jump ring mandrel.

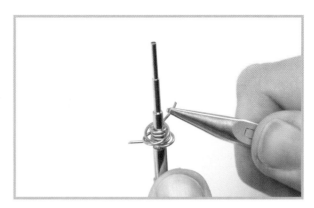

2 Switch to freeform wrapping, coiling the wire in different directions. Use the chain-nose pliers to aid your wrapping.

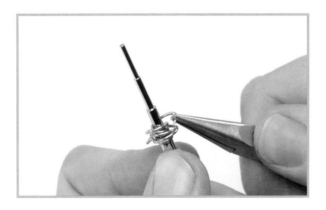

3 Using the chain-nose pliers, bend the wire ends at a 90-degree angle and push the ends down into the coil center.

4 Slide the coil off the mandrel and place it on the bench block. Hammer it a couple times to compress the outer wires; be careful not to collapse the center coil.

Repeat steps 1–4 to make 13 more small wire beads, for a total of 14.

Repeat steps 1–4 to make 4 large wire beads with a 9" (23cm) length of wire for each bead.

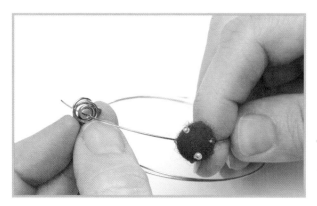

5 String a small felt ball onto the end of the memory wire. Use pressure and a little wiggling to work the wire through the ball.

6 Follow the ball with a small memory-wire bead.

7 Continue stringing balls in the following size and quantities: 3 small, 1 medium, 9 small, 1 medium, 4 small. After each small ball, string a small wire bead, unless the next bead is a medium ball, in which case you should substitute a large wire bead. Both the large balls are framed with the large wire beads. Do not string a wire bead after the very last ball.

8 Trim the wire with the memory-wire cutters. Using the glue, adhere the bead caps to each end of the wire. Allow the glue to dry completely before wearing the bracelet.

CROCHETED CIRCLE EARRINGS

This clever adaptation of crocheting in the round uses 26-gauge colored wire to create vibrant, lightweight earrings. The center of the earring is formed with a 12-gauge, colored aluminum wire jump ring that is strong enough to withstand the multiple ins and outs of the crochet hook. Colorful magatama and faceted beads are embedded into the stitches to add sparkle and whimsy.

MATERIALS

22-gauge pink wire (Artistic Wire)

26-gauge pink wire (Artistic Wire)

26-gauge red wire (Artistic Wire)

2 6mm jump rings made with 12-gauge bright pink aluminum wire (Darice) (see page 14)

20 teal/green magatama beads

20 3mm orange faceted round beads

2 3mm fuchsia faceted round beads

TOOLS

metal-tipped D 3.0mm crochet hook (Clover)

ring mandrel

round-nose pliers

chain-nose pliers

flush cutters

jeweler's hammer

bench block

sanding stick

Finished dangle length: 1¼" (3cm)

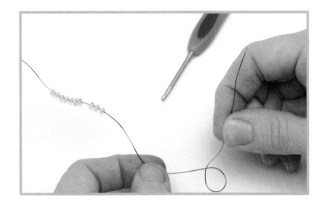

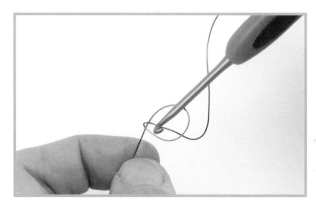

1 String 10 teal/green beads onto the pink 26-gauge wire, working directly from the spool. Beginning 2" (5cm) from the end of the wire, form the wire into a circle.

2 Bring the right-hand wire down behind the circle so it creates a line through the middle. Use the crochet hook to pull the wire up through the center of the circle. The wire will form a small loop. You just completed the first stitch on the hook.

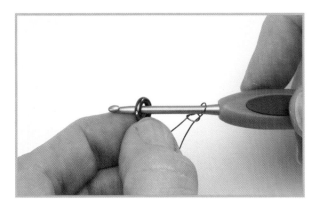

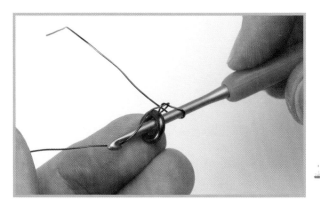

3 Place the hook through the center of a jump ring.

4 Bring the wire over the top of the ring and wrap the wire around the end of the hook.

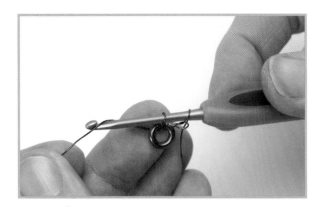

5 Bring the hook back out of the jump ring, pulling the wire through. Wrap the wire around the hook once more

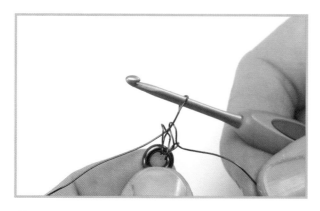

6 Bring the hook and the wire back through both the stitches on the hook.

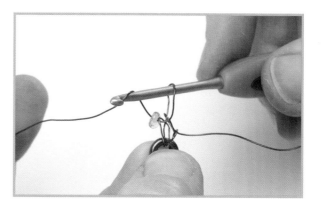

7 Slide a bead against the last stitch. Wrap the wire around the hook and pull it through the stitch a final time. (This completes the first modified double crochet stitch. It sets the pattern and height so the remaining 9 double crochet stitches are conventional.)

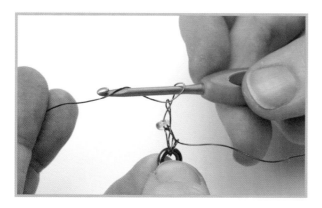

8 To begin the next stitch, wrap the wire around the hook.

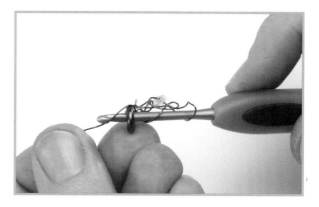

9 Place the hook through the jump ring. Bring the wire over the top of the ring and wrap it around the hook.

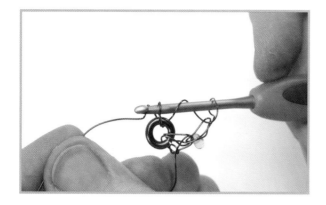

10 Pull the hook and the wire out of the ring. Wrap the wire around the hook.

11 Bring the hook and the wire through 2 of the stitches on the hook. You should be left with 2 stitches on the hook.

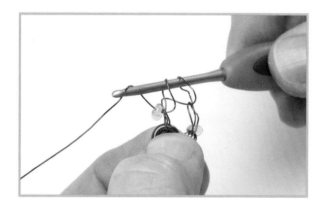

12 Slide the bead next to the new stitch, and wrap the hook with the wire. Pull the new wrap through the 2 last stitches.

13 Repeat steps 8–12 to make 8 more beaded double crochet stitches.
Place the hook through the first stitch, wrap the hook with the wire and bring it back through all the stitches on the hook to connect the circle.

14 Using the flush cutters, cut the wire off the spool with 1" (2.5cm) extra. Pass the end through the last stitch and pull the wire tight. Wrap the wire end a couple times before trimming it.

15 Use the 22-gauge pink wire to stitch the orange faceted bead to the top of each of the 10 double crochet stitches. Use your fingers to weave the wire in and out of the spaces left by the crocheted wire, adding an orange bead before the next pass.

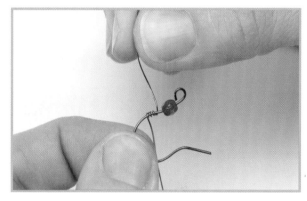

16 Twist the wire ends together before trimming the excess wire with the flush cutters.
Repeat steps 1–16 to make a matching dangle.

17 Create an earwire with the 22-gauge wire (see Making Earwires on page 13). String a pink faceted bead onto the wire end before turning it up. Wrap the 26-gauge red wire 4 times around the top of the fuchsia bead to hold it in place.

18 Attach an earwire to each finished crocheted circle.

Chapter 4

COILED AND SPIRALED

This chapter is the perfect place to get a feel for wire work and try your hand with a variety of wire types and gauges. Coiling and spiraling are not only beginner-friendly techniques, they're also core jewelry-making techniques. Spiraling the wire instantly makes a decorative wire end and also creates the open-hook portion of a clasp. Coiling wire is used to form beads and strengthen and embellish projects.

Coiling wire is simply wrapping straight wire around a perfectly round form—either another wire, a jump ring maker or a Coiling Gizmo rod—and is similar to the first step of making jump rings. The technique is the same regardless of what size wire you use. Thinner gauge coils often need to be paired with heavier gauge wire to make functional jewelry. Colorful, thin wire repeatedly coils around the hoop base to add interest and dimension to *Peace Earrings* (page 109). The 20- and 22-gauge wires used in both the *Ice Blue Coiled Bangle* (page 116) and the *Coiled Bead Bangle* (page 106) gain their strength and structure from heavy wire cores.

Spiraling wire begins with forming the end into a small loop that increases its circular shape, strength and size with each new rotation. It takes practice to regulate the tension and plier position to make a consistent spiral. The *Spiraled Wire and Ceramic Bead Bracelet* (page 100) is a series of handformed, repetitive spiral links. In the *Spiraled Resin Bracelet* (page 112), the wire spirals easily around the bead to form them into connectors and dangles.

Some of my favorite projects in this chapter marry both techniques in a single project. Heavyweight wire instantly spirals and coils to make the stunning *Glass Flower Ring* (page 119) and the *Glass Cane Ring* (page 121). The *Silver Spring Charm Bracelet* (page 103) features a strong spring coil construction; it also showcases decorative spiraled heart and bead dangles.

No matter how you decide to use the following techniques, you'll always create intricate and fun jewelry.

SPIRALED WIRE AND CERAMIC BEAD BRACELET

This project was inspired by a high school art project my good friend Teri shared with me. I saw real value in the double-spiral construction and decided it was worthy of a redesign. I experimented with lovely Vintaj bronze wire, which easily forms spirals. The addition of low-profile ceramic beads added stability and beauty to the links. The seamless closure uses a matching Vintaj hammered ring.

MATERIALS

18-gauge nontarnish bronze
    wire (Vintaj)
12 round aqua ceramic
    beads (Halcraft)
hammered bronze ring
    ⅞" (2cm) in diameter
    (Vintaj)
Aleene's Metal & Jewelry
    Glue

TOOLS

round-nose pliers
chain-nose pliers
flush cutters
jeweler's hammer
bench block
Finished length: 7" (18cm)

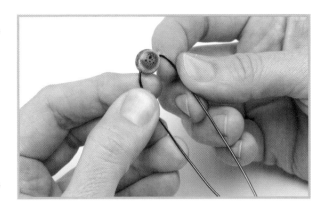

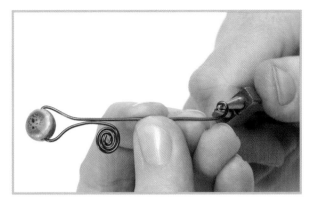

1 String a ceramic bead onto the center of a 6" (15cm) length of wire. Fold the wires down on both sides of the bead.

2 Grab the wire end with the round-nose pliers and rotate the wire around the pliers to begin making a spiral (see Making a Spiral on page 16). Make 3 complete rotations and then slide out the pliers and repeat the process to form an identical spiral with the other wire end.

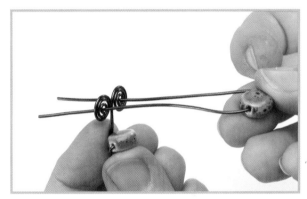

3 Use your fingertips to bend the bead down. This link becomes the hook portion of the clasp; the next link will string directly into the spirals of the hook.

4 Cut a 6" (15cm) length of wire. String a ceramic bead onto the center of the wire. Bend the wire ends down. String each wire through the center of the hook's spirals. The new bead should rest on the wire spirals.

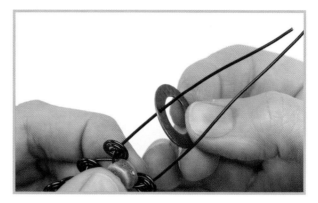

5 Grab a wire end with the round-nose pliers and spiral the wire just like in step 2. Repeat the process with the second wire end.

6 Repeat steps 4–5 to add 10 more links to the bracelet, linking each new wire through the center of the spirals from the link before.

String a bead on the eleventh wire and then bend the wire ends down. String 1 of the wires through the hole of the hammered ring.

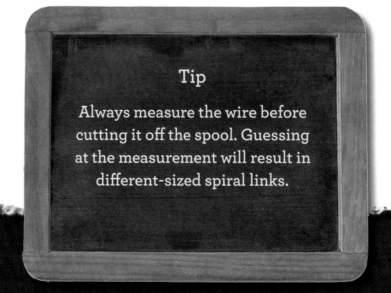

7 Bring the second wire through the inside of the ring. Spiral the ends and rest them against the front of the ring.

8 Use the jewelry glue to adhere the underside of the spirals to the front of the ring.

Tip

Always measure the wire before cutting it off the spool. Guessing at the measurement will result in different-sized spiral links.

SILVER SPRING CHARM BRACELET

This captivating bracelet pairs shiny, silver-plated wire with stunning lampwork beads. The one-of-a-kind glass beads were created specially for this project by my talented neighbor Deb Merrill—they're the perfect subject for a variety of wrap, spiral and coil wire techniques. The components are linked with sturdy springs that were quickly formed around a jump ring maker. You can find lampwork beads on Etsy, on other online stores and in local bead shops.

MATERIALS

16-gauge silver-plated copper wire (Beadsmith)

18-gauge silver-plated copper wire (Beadsmith)

3 9mm 18-gauge silver-plated jump rings (see page 14)

1 pink lentil lampwork glass bead

2 purple-and-pink round lampwork glass beads

3 green flower round lampwork glass beads

1 green doughnut lampwork glass bead

TOOLS

jump ring maker with 7mm mandrel

round-nose pliers

chain-nose pliers

bent-nose pliers

flush cutters

jeweler's hammer

bench block

Finished length: 8½" (21.5cm)

1 To form the springs, wrap the 16-gauge wire around the 7mm jump ring maker 9 times, compressing the wire as needed (see Compressing a Coil on page 15).

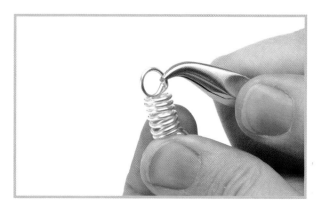

2 Slide the coils off the tool and trim both ends flush to the coil. Use the bent-nose pliers to bend the first and last rings to a 90-degree angle from the top and bottom of the coil. Repeat steps 1–2 to make 3 more coils, for a total of 4 coils.

3 Cut three 7" (18cm) pieces of 18-gauge wire to create spiral-wrapped beads (see Making Wrapped Links on page 17) with the pink lentil bead, a green lampwork glass bead and a purple-and-pink glass bead.

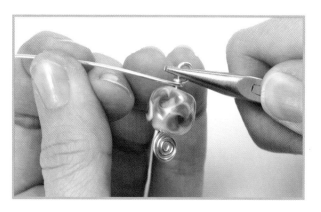

4 Cut a 5" (13cm) length of 18-gauge wire to make a spiral dangle. Grab the wire end with the round-nose pliers and tightly rotate the wire around it (see Making a Spiral on page 16). Make a total of 4 rotations and then pinch the wire with the chain-nose pliers to bend it at a 90-degree angle. Hammer the spiral to harden the metal. String on a green flower bead. Form the top of the wire into a loop. Wrap the wire end around the base of the loop. Use the flush cutters to trim the excess wire.

Repeat step 4 to make 2 more spiral dangles, 1 with a purple-and-pink lampwork bead and the other with a green flower bead.

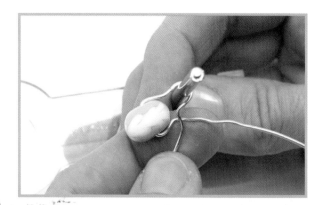

5 Cut a 5" (13cm) length of 18-gauge wire and string the green doughnut bead onto the wire. Wrap 1 end of the wire around the jump ring maker mandrel to create a hanging loop.

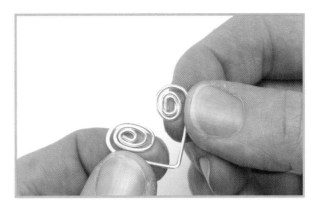

6   Grasp the loop with the chain-nose pliers and wrap the other wire end 3 times around the base of the hanging loop to secure it. Trim away any excess wire with the flush cutters.

7   Cut a 5" (13cm) length of 18-gauge wire. Grab 1 of the wire ends with round-nose pliers and make a spiral, rotating the wire around the pliers 3 times. Repeat for the other end of the wire. Bend the center of the wire in half to make a heart. Hammer the wire to harden the metal.

8   Make two 1¼" (3cm) long S-links using the 16-gauge wire (see Making an S-Loop/Link on page 16). Hammer the S-link to harden the wire. One of these will be part of the clasp.

Connect the components in the following sequence: spring, wrapped lentil bead, jump ring strung with two spiral bead dangles (one pink, the other green; see Opening and Closing Jump Rings on page 15), spring, S-link, wrapped green bead, jump ring strung with a spiral dangle (green flower bead) and a green doughnut dangle, spring, pink-and-purple spiral bead, spring linked with heart dangle, S-link.

9   String a 9mm jump ring through the small loops around the center of the S-link (this will help stabilize the link and prevent the components from coming off). Leave the S-link at the end of the bracelet free so it can function as the clasp, hooking into the loop at the end of a spring.

COILED BEAD BANGLE

The Coiling Gizmo effortlessly transforms straight wire into perfectly formed coils. It's so easy to use you'll be amazed how quickly you can form both the wire beads and long-coil portion of this bangle. You'll have a lot of fun creating these quick components. Just don't get dizzy!

MATERIALS

16-gauge silver-colored
     copper wire
20-gauge silver-colored
     copper wire
22-gauge blue-colored
     copper wire
24-gauge silver-colored
     wire
2 4mm round silver beads
1 12mm round maroon
     Lucite bead
1 9mm green glass bead
1 10mm millefiori bead

TOOLS

Coiling Gizmo
round-nose pliers
chain-nose pliers
flush cutters
jeweler's hammer
bench block

Finished size: 8½" (21.5cm)

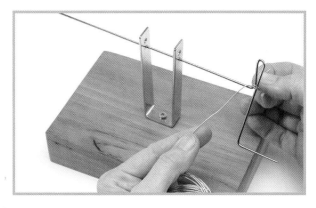

1 Set up the Coiling Gizmo according to the package directions (I anchored mine to a heavy piece of wood). The Coiling Gizmo comes with 2 different-sized rods. To begin with, use the smaller rod. Hook the 20-gauge wire end around the handle.

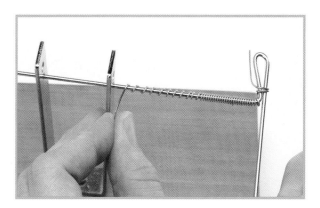

2 Begin winding the wire around the rod to make a 4½" (11.5cm) length of coil.

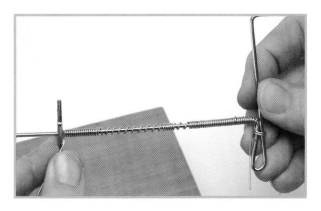

3 Push the handle firmly against the base to condense the coil.

4 Unwrap the wire end from the handle. With the flush cutters, trim the wire close at the beginning and end of the coil. Set the coil aside until you string the bracelet.

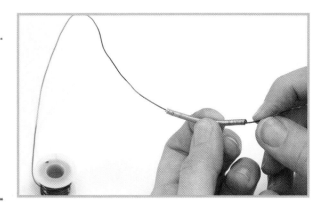

5 To make the silver coil bead, repeat steps 1–4 with the 24-gauge silver wire to wind a 1½" (4cm) long coil. String the finished silver coil onto the blue wire.

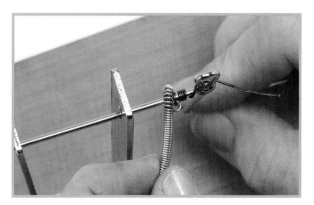

6 Make 4 rotations of the blue wire on the Coiling Gizmo. Then make 4 more rotations with the added silver coil.

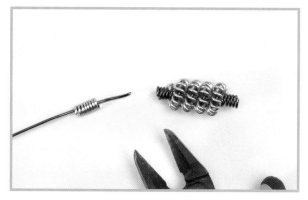

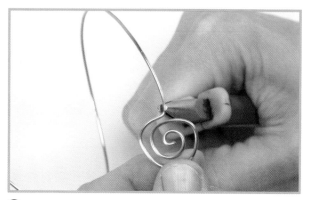

7 Finish the bead with 4 more single blue rotations. Use the flush cutters to trim both the excess blue wire and silver coil.

Repeat steps 4–7 to make a larger blue coil bead, but this time make a 1½" (4cm) coil of blue wire, and string it onto the 20-gauge silver wire. When making the coiled bead, make only 3 rotations with the silver wire, the added blue coil and the silver wire before cutting the wire off the spool.

8 Cut a 15" (38cm) length of 16-gauge wire. Grab 1 end of the wire with the round-nose pliers and rotate the wire to create an open spiral (see Making a Spiral on page 16). Make 3 rotations. Adjust the spiral to your liking, leaving enough of an opening in the outer loop for a hook to link to. Use the pliers to turn the wire under the spiral to a 90-degree angle.

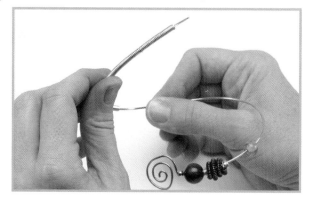

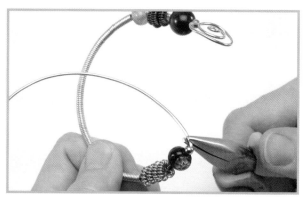

9 Bend the remaining wire into a rounded wrist shape. String the following sequence onto the wire: silver bead, Lucite bead, blue coiled bead, green glass bead, 4½" (11.5cm) silver coil, silver coil bead, millefiori bead, silver bead.

10 Test fit the bracelet before bending the wire backward at a 90-degree angle to hold the strung beads in place.

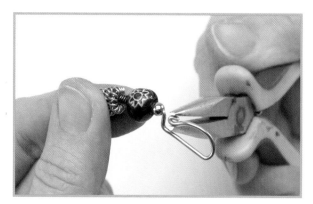

11 Create a ½" (1.5cm) hook by bending the wire 90-degrees to hold the beads in place. Bend the wire 90 degrees again and then use the round-nose pliers to make a bend about ½" (1.5cm) from the second 90-degree bend. Trim away the excess wire and then fold up the wire end of the hook, pressing the wire end with the chain-nose pliers, to create a smooth finish.

12 Hammer the hook and spiral to harden the metal.

PEACE EARRINGS

This was a challenging project to design because I struggled to find the perfect marriage of wire gauges. I'm thrilled with the results; these earrings were well worth all the discarded efforts in my studio trash. I've eliminated the guess-work; stick to the specified wire gauges, and you should be able to quickly recreate a perfect pair of earrings. Here's hoping that peace stays in style.

MATERIALS
20-gauge silver-colored wire (Artistic Wire)
24-gauge brown-colored wire (Artistic Wire)
24-gauge orange-colored wire (Artistic Wire)
2 silver metal heart charms (Plaid)

TOOLS
ring mandrel
round-nose pliers
chain-nose pliers
bent-nose pliers
flush cutters
jeweler's hammer
bench block
sanding stick

Finished dangle length: ⅞" (2cm)

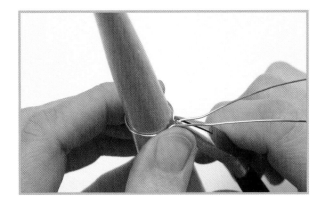

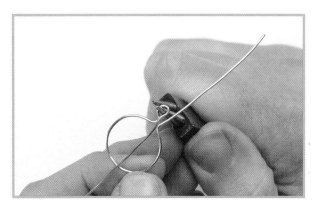

1 Cut an 8" (20.5cm) length of 20-gauge silver wire, and wrap the middle of the wire around the center of the ring mandrel to create a hoop. Bend one of the wires up to a 90-degree angle. Slide the hoop off the mandrel.

2 Wrap the bent wire around the end of the round-nose pliers to shape it into a hanging loop. Turn the wire end to fall straight down to intersect the middle of the hoop. This wire creates the center line of the peace sign.

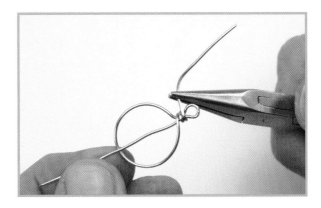

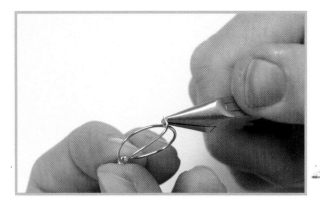

3 Wrap the second wire a couple times around the base of the hanging loop to hold it in place. Trim away any excess wire with the flush cutters. Using the chain-nose pliers, press the cut end flush against the base of the hanging loop.

4 Trim the end of the intersecting wire ⅛" (3mm) below the hoop. Us the chain-nose pliers to bend it up behind the hoop base.

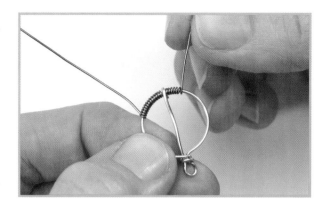

5 Cut a 16" (40.5cm) length of brown 24-gauge wire. Wrap the center of the brown wire just beside the intersecting wire at the base of the hoop. Tightly wrap the brown wire around the hoop, working your way one-third up one side. If necessary, use bent-nose pliers to squeeze the wraps close together (see Compressing a Coil on page 15).

Repeat the process to wrap the other half of the brown wire one-third up the other side of the hoop base. Use the flush cutters to trim off the excess wire.

6 Cut a 1¼" (3cm) length of 20-gauge silver wire. Use the chain-nose pliers to bend the center of the wire at a 45-degree angle. Position the folded wire over the center line of the hoop. Wrap the wire ends around the sides of the hoop, using the chain-nose pliers to help press in the wire ends.

7 Cut a 22" (56cm) length of 24-gauge orange wire and begin wrapping it alongside one of the side silver wires, as you did in step 5.

8 Continue wrapping the sides of the hoop until you reach the ends of the bent silver wire.
Repeat steps 1–8 to make a second peace hoop.

9 Use the ring mandrel to shape two 2" (5cm) lengths of 20-gauge wire into earwires (see Making Earwires on page 13). Attach a finished peace hoop and a heart charm onto each earwire.

SPIRALED RESIN BRACELET

Like a bright strand of gumdrops, these vibrant resin beads are eye candy for your wrist. This projects uses two different wrapping techniques: One wraps a bead and forms loops on either end so it can be linked to the next bead; the other transforms the bead into a caged dangle. Pairing both techniques creates a strong linked bracelet with whimsical decorative dangles.

MATERIALS

20-gauge silver-colored copper wire (ColourCraft)

18-gauge silver-colored copper wire (ColourCraft)

2 6mm jump rings made with 18-gauge silver wire (see page 14)

3 14mm turquoise round resin beads (Fresh by Plaid)

3 14mm red round resin beads (Fresh by Plaid)

3 14mm purple round resin beads (Fresh by Plaid)

2 16mm round orange resin beads (Fresh by Plaid)

3 16mm round purple resin beads (Fresh by Plaid)

3 16mm round yellow resin beads (Fresh by Plaid)

TOOLS

ring mandrel

round-nose pliers

bent-nose pliers

chain-nose pliers

flush cutters

jeweler's hammer

bench block

Finished length: 8½" (21.5cm)

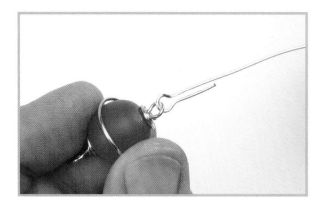

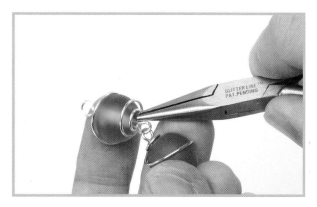

1 Make a spiral-wrapped bead (see Making Wrapped Links on page 17) with a 7" (18cm) length of 20-gauge wire and a red resin bead.

Form a loop in a new 7" (18cm) section of wire, and thread it through a loop on the wrapped red bead.

2 Slide on a 14mm turquoise bead, and make another wrapped bead.

3 Repeat steps 1–2 seven more times, adding the following sequence of 14mm resin beads: purple, red, turquoise, purple, red, turquoise, purple.

To make the large bead dangle, cut a 7" (18cm) length of wire. Form the wire into a loop as you did in step 1. This time, hook the new wire loop onto the connector loop of the first red spiraled bead. Slide the 16mm purple bead onto the long wire end.

4 Use the chain-nose pliers to bend the wire flat against the bead where it emerges from the hole. Then spiral the wire up around the bead. Wrap the end around the base of the loop.

Repeat the process to attach 7 more 16mm dangles at each spiraled bead connection. Place them in the following color sequence: yellow, orange, purple, yellow, orange, purple, yellow.

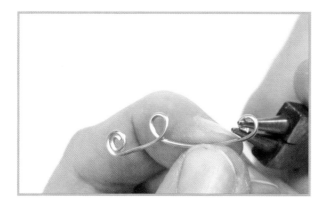

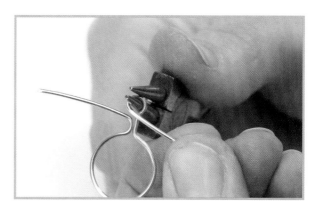

5 Cut a 2" (5cm) piece of 18-gauge wire to make a 1" (2.5cm) toggle clasp. Grasp the wire with the middle of the round-nose pliers. Fold the wire in half, crossing one side over the other to make a loop. Use the round-nose pliers to grasp the ends of the wire to spiral them (see Making a Spiral on page 16).

6 Use the 18-gauge wire to make a ⅝" (1.5cm) diameter, single-wrapped O-ring (see Making Hook and O-Ring Clasps on page 19). Wrap the wire around the small end of the ring mandrel to make the ⅝" (1.5cm) loop. Fold both wires down to a 90-degree angle. Create a connecting loop by wrapping one of the wires around the round-nose pliers.

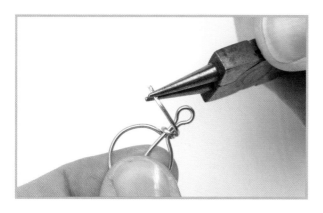

7 Secure both loops by wrapping the connecting section with the second wire. Trim the wire ends with the flush cutters. Hammer the spiral toggle and O-ring to harden the metal.

8 Use a jump ring and the chain-nose pliers to connect the O-ring to one end of the bracelet (see Opening and Closing Jump Rings on page 15).

9 Use a second jump ring to connect the toggle to the other side of the bracelet.

ICE BLUE COILED BANGLE

Impress your friends with this project. I guarantee they'll have no idea how you made it! The secret is two continuous strands of beaded and coiled wire, one silver and one ice blue. The finished strands are alternately strung onto the heavyweight 16-gauge wire. Add interest to the finished project by incorporating an assortment of small charms, message tags and beads.

MATERIALS

16-gauge silver-colored wire

22-gauge ice-blue wire (Artistic Wire)

22-gauge silver-colored wire (Artistic Wire)

15 assorted turquoise glass beads

3 10mm × 8mm iridescent white glass beads (Darice)

6 10mm iridescent lentil glass beads (Halcraft)

5 6mm × 8mm faceted rondelle turquoise glass beads

4 silver charms (Darice)

3 tag message charms (Plaid)

TOOLS

jump ring mandrel

chain-nose pliers

flush cutters

Finished length: 8½" (21.5cm)

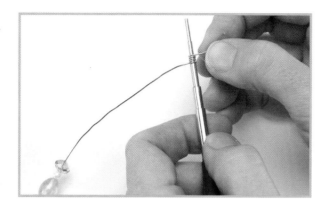

1 Unroll a 3' (3m) of the 22-gauge blue wire from the spool. Slide a random assortment of 18 beads and charms onto the wire. Starting at the end of the wire, coil the wire end 5 times around the 3mm section of the jump ring mandrel. Slide the coiled wire off the mandrel.

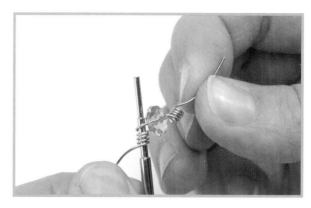

2 Slide 1 of the strung beads up against the coil. Position the mandrel ½" (1.5cm) down from the first coil. Using the wire from the spool, wrap the wire 5 times around the mandrel again. The coils will hold the bead in place.

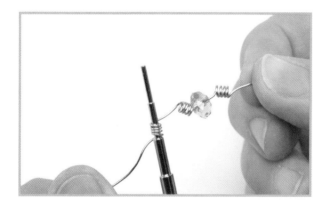

3 Leave ½" (1.5cm) of straight wire and then make another coil.

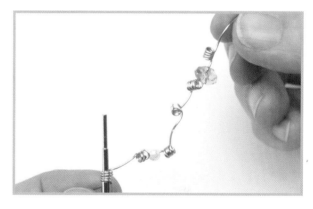

4 Repeat steps 2–3 along the length of the wire.
The pattern should be coil, bead, coil, ½" (1.5cm) straight wire, coil, ½" (1.5cm) straight wire, repeat. After all the beads have been coiled in place, leave ½" (1.5cm) of straight wire, and make a last coil before trimming the wire off the spool.
Repeat steps 1–4 with the 22-gauge silver wire.

5 Cut a 12" (30.5cm) length of the 16-gauge wire. Working with the chain-nose pliers, shape one end of the wire into a 1" (2.5cm) long rectangular hook clasp.

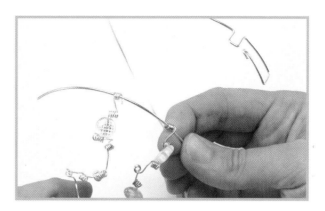

6 Bend the base of the hook to a 90-degree angle. Bend it 3 more times to form a U-shape with squared corners.

7 Begin stringing the first coil of the blue wire onto the open end of the 16-gauge core wire. Follow it with the first coil of the silver wire.

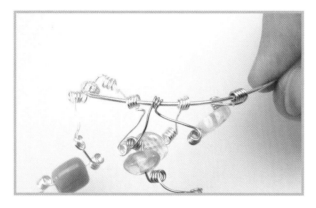

8 Continue stringing the unbeaded coils, alternating the silver with the blue.

9 Tightly compress the strung wires so they measure approximately 7½" (19cm). Test fit the bangle around your wrist; release some of the tension in the coiled wire sections if you need more length. The coiled beaded sections should protrude ½" (1.5cm) from the 16-gauge core wire. When you find the suitable length, use the chain-nose pliers to make a 90-degree bend in the 16-gauge wire. After ½" (1.5cm), bend the wire to a 90-degree angle.

10 Use the chain-nose pliers to shape the end into a 1" (2.5cm) long, ½" (1.5cm) wide rectangular loop. Secure the loop by wrapping the wire end three times around the base of the rectangle. Trim the excess wire with the flush cutters.

GLASS FLOWER RING

his project is for those who need instant gratification. In minutes, a single bead and length of wire wrap and twist to create a beautiful ring. The trick is to find a low-profile bead that will sit flat against your hand and has a large enough opening to accommodate a double thickness of 18-gauge wire. Cathi Milligan of Beadbrains created a stunning flower bead that is the perfect fit for this project.

MATERIALS

18-gauge silver-colored wire
center-drilled lamp work
    flower bead (Beadbrains
    by Cathi Milligan)

TOOLS

ring mandrel
chain-nose pliers
flush cutters
tape or pen (see step 1)

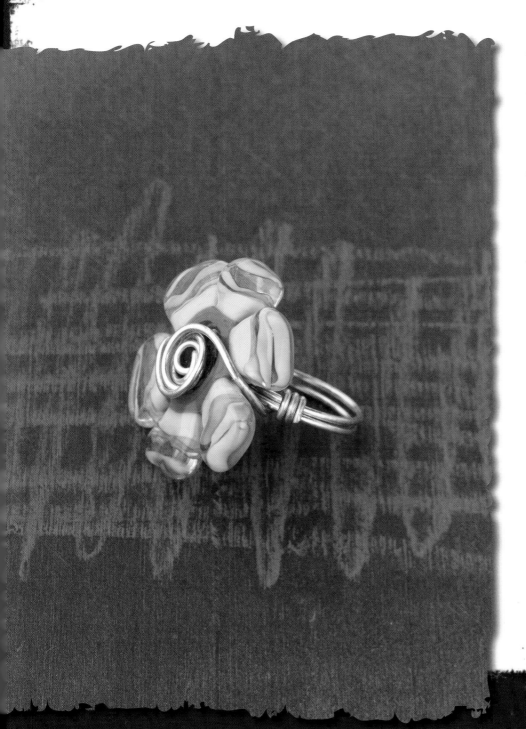

 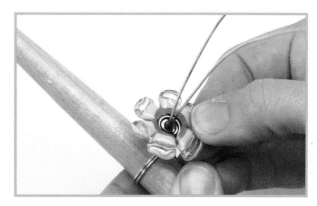

1 To determine your ring size, slide a favorite ring onto the mandrel and mark the position (with tape on a metal mandrel or pen on a wooden one).

Cut a 16" (40.5cm) length of the 18-gauge wire. Wrap the center of the wire completely around the marked section of the mandrel and then bring both wire ends back around to the front. You have made a double-banded ring. Use the chain-nose pliers to bend the wires to a 90-degree angle where they meet.

2 Slide the glass flower onto both wires so it rests directly on top of the ring band.

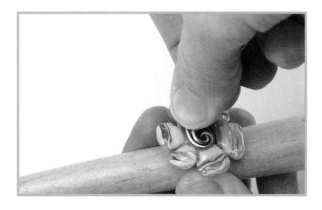 

3 Holding both wires in your hand, rotate them 2 times around the center of the bead so they form a spiral.

4 Separate the wires. Thread one through a break in the petals on the left side and the other wire through a break in the petals on the right side.

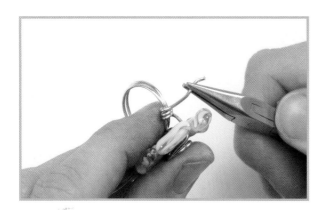

5 Slide the ring off the mandrel. Tightly wrap each wire 2–3 times around the double ring band. Use the flush cutters to trim the wires. Use the chain-nose pliers to press the cut wire ends flat against the ring band.

GLASS CANE RING

This flexible ring design allows you to form a focal point with a combination of any three beads. The structure of the ring is formed with 18-gauge wire; a separate 20-gauge wire adds embellishment and connects your beads to the center of the ring.

MATERIALS

16-gauge silver-colored wire
20-gauge silver-colored wire
3 orange cane flower beads
(Blue Moon Beads)
2 silver flat bead spacers

TOOLS

ring mandrel
round-nose pliers
chain-nose pliers
flush cutters
jeweler's hammer
bench block
tape or pen (see step 1)

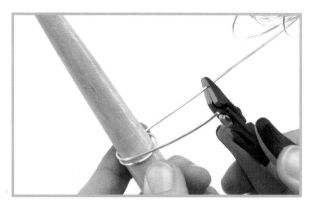

1 To determine your ring size, slide a favorite ring onto the mandrel and mark the position (with tape for a metal mandrel or pen for a wooden one).

Cut an 8" (20cm) length of the 16-gauge wire. Wrap the center of the wire completely around the marked section of the mandrel and then bring both wire ends back around to the front. Let the wire ends extend out from the sides so the sides and back are double-banded, but also so the front is approximately ¾" (2cm) a single thickness of wire. Using the flush cutters, trim the wires so they are 1½" (4cm) long.

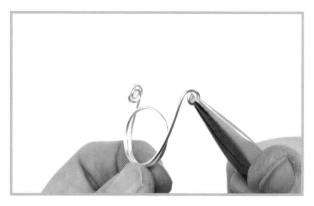

2 Using the round-nose pliers, form the ends of the wires into spirals (see Making a Spiral on page 16).

3 Slide the ring band off the mandrel. Gently hammer the spiral ends on the bench block to harden them.

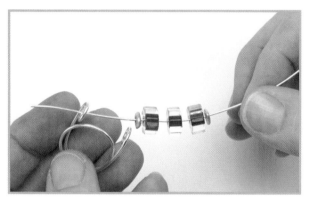

4 Cut a 5" (13cm) length of 20-gauge wire. String one end of the 20-gauge wire through one spiral. String a bead spacer, the 3 flower beads and the second spacer. String the wire through the second spiral.

5 Center the wire so an equal amount of the wire extends out either side of the spirals. Wrap each wire end 5 times around the single wire shank on both sides of the ring.

6 Wrap the wire 3 times around the double-wire band. Use the flush cutters to trim the excess wire. Use the chain-nose pliers to press the cut ends flat against the band.

BEADED COIL EARRINGS

These earrings showcase the amazing capabilities of wire. With the help of the Coiling Gizmo, beaded purple wire forms intricate wire beads. Silver wire suspends the wire beads while also acting as functional earring findings. If you don't have the time to make the coiled beads, you can always substitute a pair of purchased beads. The dynamic shape of the earring findings will give you stunning results.

MATERIALS

20-gauge German-style silver-colored copper wire (Beadalon)

22-gauge German-style silver-colored copper wire (Beadalon)

24-gauge purple wire (Artistic Wire)

11/10 seed beads in amethyst purple, metallic purple and raspberry

TOOLS

Coiling Gizmo
round-nose pliers
chain-nose pliers
flush cutters
sanding stick

Finished dangle length: 1¾" (4.5cm)

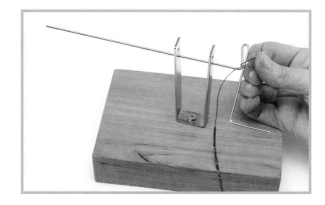

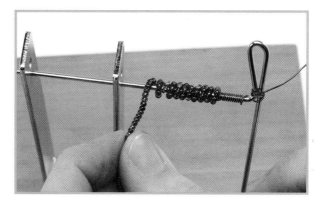

1 Working from the spool of 24-gauge purple wire, string approximately 15" (38cm) of seed beads. Wrap the wire end around the handle end of the Coiling Gizmo's small winding rod.

2 Wind the handle to coil approximately ½" (1.5cm) of the purple wire. Push the beads up to the coil and turn the handle to make 2½" (6.5cm) of beaded coil. Untie the wire from the Coiling Gizmo and slip the beaded coil off the winding rod.

3 Working from the spool, string the beaded coil onto the 20-gauge wire. Wrap the 24-gauge wire ends around the 20-gauge wire 3 times to prevent the seed beads from sliding off. Use the flush cutters to trim the excess wire.

4 Wrap the 20-gauge wire end around the handle of the small winding rod. Wind 3 rotations of plain silver wire onto the rod. Wind 4 rotations of the beaded coil and silver wire together.

5 If you have extra beaded coil, cut the purple wire and slide the excess beads out of the way, rewrapping the end of the purple wire onto the silver wire.

6 Make 4 more rotations of just the silver wire.

7 Cut the silver wire off the spool. Unwrap the wire from the Coiling Gizmo handle and slide the coiled bead off the arm. Using the flush cutters, trim the silver wires close to the coils. Twist the finished bead counterclockwise to shape it into a round bead.

8 String the coil bead onto the 22-gauge wire. Let it slide down against the spool. Use the chain-nose pliers to create a fold ¾" (2cm) from the end of the wire (this marks the top of the earring). Create a second fold 1½" (4cm) down from the first to mark the base of the earring.

9 Slide the coil bead up against the last fold. Bend the wire 1" (2.5cm) from the last fold. Leave a 1¾" (3cm) length of straight wire, forming the wire into a loop around the end of the round-nose pliers.

10 Wrap the wire around the base of the loop 3 times. Using the flush cutters, trim the wire off the spool at the base of the wrap. Thread the beginning of the wire into the loop. Use the chain-nose pliers to bend the last ¼" (6mm) up at an angle so the wire ends stay linked together. Sand the earring (see Basic Wire Finishing on page 20.)

Repeat steps 1–10 to create a matching earring.

RESOURCES

BEADALON
www.beadalon.com
German-style plated silver wire,
Artistic Wire colored copper wire,
ColourCraft Wire, Remembrance
Memory Wire, bead stringing wires,
jump ring tool, jump ring mandrel,
chasing hammer, bench block,
Coiling Gizmo, flush cutters, pliers

BEADBRAINS
www.beadbrains.com
Lampwork beads, flower beads,
lampwork heart pendant

THE BEADSMITH
www.helby.com
Silver-plated copper wire

BLUE MOON BEADS
www.creativityinc.com
Beads, wooden links, corrugated
silver metal beads

CLOVER
www.clover-usa.com
Knitting spool, crochet hooks

DARICE
www.darice.com
Beads, aluminum wire, wire jig

DUNCAN CRAFTS
www.ilovetocreate.com
Aleene's Jewelry & Metal Glue

FELTWORKS
http://needlecrafts.eksuccessbrands.com
Wool felt beads

HALCRAFT
www.halcraft.com
Beads

PLAID
www.plaidonline.com
Resin beads, resin charms, silver metal
charms, glass pendants, cuff blank

THE RING LORD
www.theringlord.com
Rubber O-rings

VINTAJ
www.vintaj.com
Brass wire, natural brass charms, lampwork beads, wooden mandrel, file set

INDEX

MORE JEWELRY INSPIRATION

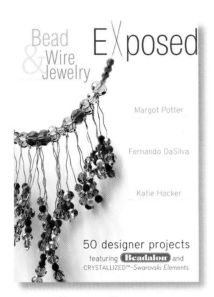

Bead and Wire Jewelry Exposed

Margot Potter, Fernando DaSilva and Katie Hacker

Bead & Wire Jewelry Exposed features over 50 high-fashion jewelry pieces made using techniques that reveal typically hidden components. Beading wire, cording, findings, tubing and chain take center stage in these clever and designs. Each of the three authors, Margot Potter, Katie Hacker and Fernando DaSilva, puts his or her spin on the exposed-element designs, so there's something for everyone.

paperback with flaps;
8.75" × 10.875";
144 pages; Z2508
ISBN-10: 1-60061-159-1
ISBN-13: 978-1-60061-159-9

Beyond the Bead

Margot Potter

If you are a restlessly creative do-it-yourself type, you've found your book. Impatient Beader Margot Potter grabs inspiration from bead making, scrapbooking and mixed-media artistry and brings it together in one book all about wearing your work. *Beyond the Bead* features 26 step-by-step jewelry projects that will teach you a variety of mixed-media techniques and show you an inspired use of supplies. Multiple variations and gallery projects will show you that creativity has no boundaries.

paperback;
8.25" × 10.875";
128 pages; Z2066
ISBN-10: 1-60061-105-2
ISBN-13: 978-1-60061-105-6

A Bead in Time

Lisa Crone

Dip into your life and memories for jewelry inspiration. In *A Bead in Time*, Lisa Crone takes you step-by-step through 35 photo-inspired jewelry projects while giving you tips on how to design pieces based on your own life. You'll learn a range of beading and jewelry techniques, including wire wrapping, peyote stitch, macramé and more. Whether you're a beading beginner or an experienced jewelry crafter, you can get started transforming life into art.

paperback;
8.25" × 10.875";
128 pages; Z2912
ISBN-10: 1-60061-310-1
ISBN-13: 978-1-60061-310-4

These and other fine North Light titles are available at your local craft retailer, bookstore or online supplier, or visit our Web site at www.mycraftivitystore.com.